HOW TO *Forgive* YOUR CHILDREN

by *Quin Sherrer*
with
Ruthanne Garlock

Aglow Publications
A Ministry of Women's Aglow Fellowship, Int'l.
P.O. Box 1548
Lynnwood, WA 98046-1558
USA

Cover photo by Robert Charter
Cover calligraphy by Katherine Malmsten

Unless otherwise noted, all scripture quotations in this publication are from the Holy Bible, New International Version. Copyright © 1973, 1978, 1984, International Bible Society. Other versions are abbreviated as follows: TAB (The Amplified Bible), KJV (King James Version), TLB (The Living Bible), NASB (New American Standard Bible), NKJV (New King James Version).

ISBN 0-932305-73-3

Acknowledgements

I wish to acknowledge and thank the three pastors who patiently taught me *about* forgiving and praying:

Peter Lord
Jamie Buckingham
Forrest Mobley

And the three dear ones who have taught me most *how* to forgive and pray, by forgiving me and continuing to be my prayer warriors, my precious children:

Quinett Rae
Keith Alan
Sherry Ruth

And, of course, the priest of our home, their father and my husband and prayer partner:

LeRoy Raymond

Special thanks also to Ruthanne Garlock, my co-writer, and her patient husband, John; to my prayer partner Fran Ewing, who was also my sounding board; to Gwen Weising, *Aglow* magazine editor, who encouraged me all the way; and finally Carol Greenwood, the Aglow editor who worked with me on this project. And to *all* the many, many parents whose testimonies are shared here, my sincere gratitude and appreciation.

Quin Sherrer

NOTE

The circumstances of certain events and names of individuals and locations mentioned have been changed to protect the privacy of the individuals involved and to maintain confidentiality.

Table of Contents

Table of Contents

Foreword

Forgive My Children?

Children inflict much pain upon their parents. Some reasons for this are due to the parents and some due to the children.

Rearing children is a long and often thankless job. Parents give much of themselves in bringing their children to maturity. On that long path lie many headaches and heartaches. Often parents are accused, attacked, ignored, rebuffed, and resented by their children. If there is not constant forgiveness, there will be a storing up of resentments—a keeping of accounts of wrongs done.

Forgiveness, real forgiveness, God's forgiveness, is an absolute essential for effectively relating to God and to our children. The Bible is not clear about some things, but about forgiveness it is *absolutely* clear. Parents need to make sure they have forgiven in the same way God has granted forgiveness to them.

Two things have made forgiveness easy for me. First is the realization that I have made many mistakes in rearing my children. For these mistakes I need their forgiveness and have asked for it. Many of their wrongdoings are reactions to my mistakes.

Secondly, God forgives me for repeated attitudes and actions over a long period of time and development.

Forgiveness is important and needs to be taken seriously. LeRoy and Quin Sherrer's relationship with their children makes this book on forgiveness one written out of life.

It was a joy to be the Sherrers' pastor and discipler. I am glad God let me relate to this family. I know this book will bring life to others.

Peter M. Lord

Introduction

How do you suppose Eve felt when she learned Cain, her beloved first-born—the first "born" man on earth—had killed her precious second son, Abel? Can't you imagine her feelings? Heartbroken, hurt, grieved, utterly crushed, and disappointed by her own child.

Ever since Eve's time, other Abels and Cains have been stepping on their parents' hearts. These parents, too, have been overwhelmed by these same painful feelings.

Since the publication of my book, *How to Pray for Your Children*, I've had the opportunity to travel across North America, speaking to women and praying for hurting mothers. I've discovered a disheartening fact: Mothers (and fathers, too) often have a hard time with the hurts they've suffered from their children. It's as if those wounds never quite heal. The parents, blinded by the pain, overlook the one step they must take to free themselves and restore the broken relationship. That step? *Forgiveness*.

One evening recently as my son Keith and I sat on the side of his bed talking, he asked me a pertinent question. "Mom, do you know what triggered my return to the Lord? It's something you can share with other mothers."

"What?" I asked, my curiosity aroused.

"Things began to turn around the night I called you and Dad and asked you to forgive me," he said. I remembered. Shortly after he graduated from college and had started his first full-time job as a graphic artist, he dialed us from a pay phone outside the hotel conference room where, on the encouragement of his boss, he was enrolled in a success seminar. He talked to me first, then to his dad. Each of us responded with the same words, "Keith, I forgive you."

"Even the secular world knows the necessity of forgiveness," Keith said that night. "In the seminar, they told us forgiveness is one way to prevent stress or sickness. Of course, they didn't tell us about the peace only Jesus can give—because they didn't know about it."

God used that secular seminar to help Keith identify his need to ask our forgiveness. At the same time, the Holy Spirit's eraser completely removed from my memory what Keith's offense was. His dad can't remember either. Isn't that like the Lord? Not only did we forgive, we forgot. What is more, our son was set free.

This book is about a lot of parents like you and me and how they have dealt with the pain and hurts in their relationships with their children. It is about dealing deathblows to unforgiveness, whether it's toward their own children, adopted children, step-children, in-law children, wayward children, or toward their parents. I've included interviews with parents who've opened their hearts and expressed to me their honest hurt and pain in their relationships with their children. Some have said: "My child has put me through things too painful to discuss."

"I've kept my hurts locked up, just between God and me."

"I struggle to accept that our family is in a crisis because just one child has gone astray."

"I've always dreamed my son would be a Catholic priest—now he's a student in a Protestant Bible school. I'm so disappointed in him."

"It is God who judges, God who forgives, and God who gives me the stamina to go on living."

"Overwhelming grief. . .that's what my daughter has put me through."

"I tell myself I must not care what other people think; but I'm human, and I do care."

"When I hear Christians viciously attacking homosexuals, I want to stand up and scream, 'You're talking about my son! You'll never win them if you can't love them!' "

We are now generations past Adam and Eve, yet daily we continue to face the need to forgive within the framework of our families. May God help us implement the scriptural how-tos of forgiveness and encourage us to face what He requires of us—to make forgiveness a lifestyle. Not only will we experience God's peace, but our children will be free to be all He created them to be.

Quin Sherrer
Destin, Florida

One

Why Forgive?

Connie came home from work early one Tuesday afternoon and discovered her high school son in bed with his girlfriend.

"What do you mean?" she screamed at the terrified girl. "You have no right to defile my home like this! Get out of my house."

"Rob, I'll deal with you later. Get up and go mow that grass I told you to cut yesterday."

Fleeing to the bathroom, Connie sat on the edge of the tub, shaking and fighting to control her anger. How long had this been going on? How could she ever forgive Rob for stooping so low, especially in his own house? She was furious.

"Raising a teenager as a single parent is a lot more than I bargained for," she moaned. "Oh, God, help!"

• • • • •

Emma and Stuart have repeatedly forgiven their oldest son, but they have just about given up. A junkie, he has stolen almost everything of value from their home—money, a gun collection, sterling silver flatware, and a stereo. How much more forgiveness can parents give?

. . . . .

Mattie's son spent three years overseas with the military, married a Korean, had a little boy, then decided to stay. Reared in a middle-class New England home where he never wanted for anything, he now shares a primitive home with twelve of his wife's relatives and has apparently abandoned his American family.

Mattie hurts most over the silent years since her son last wrote. Though she's repeatedly written to ask his forgiveness for anything she might have done to hurt him, she still has no idea why he has rejected her.

"Do you know what it's like never to get a birthday card or a Christmas letter?" she asked me plaintively. "No consideration! No thought to all the nights I worry and wonder about him. Forgive him? Why?"

. . . . .

These hurting parents, facing up to the deep wounds inflicted by their children, know God requires them to forgive. Yet they struggle. Their minds, like those of millions of parents who have wrestled with similar circumstances, ring with the same question: Why? Why should we extend forgiveness to those who have hurt us so deeply?

In this chapter we will explore *why* we must forgive and *how* we can do it God's way.

A Journey to Forgiveness

First, let me tell you the story of a widow named Gloria who experienced her own journey of forgiveness. I've rarely met anyone whose countenance exuded such peace; yet her life had been anything but peaceful. Her pilgrimage began late one night with a phone call from her married daughter, Lisa.

"Mom, can you come get the baby and me?" Lisa asked anxiously. "Randall just came in high and wild. I'm afraid he might do something crazy. I'd feel safer spending the night with you."

"Okay, Honey," Gloria replied. "Your brother just got in on the bus; I'll have him drive me right over. Sure you'll be all right until we get there? What about going to your neighbors?"

"I don't want to involve my new neighbors, Mom, but come as soon as you can. Maybe I can get Randall calmed down and in bed. Hurry!"

When Gloria arrived at her daughter's mobile home on the outskirts of town, she heard loud shouts and arguing. Her son jumped out of the car and raced to the front door. Before he got there, Randall opened fire on him. The bullet hit him square in the chest and the young marine fell to the ground dead as his mother watched, horrified.

It's been eight years since Gloria's youngest son, just home on military leave, was murdered by her son-in-law. A judicial technicality kept Randall out of prison, but Lisa divorced him and asked Gloria to raise their baby. Life became more difficult when Lisa moved in with a man and had two more babies. Tension mounted again when Gloria's younger daughter married someone Gloria disapproved of and they also had two children.

Forgiveness Brings Peace

Gloria faced up to the fact that she could not continue dwelling on her son-in-law's horrendous crime. Doing so would only keep her chained to her resentment. She recognized her own inability to forgive, and she asked for the Lord's help. Immediately it came to her that she must release her anger and resentment to God. She began by telling the Lord her deepest, most painful feelings. Some she had never admitted before—ugly, angry feelings. In doing so, the picture became clearer; she "owned up" to her feelings, seeing her reaction as sinful. At that point, Gloria asked God to forgive her; and then she forgave her daughter from her heart. She made a decision to forgive.

"I saw that my bitterness and resentment infected our whole family. My daughters were mad at me; I was mad at them. I had to forgive and stop looking back. When I did, we began talking again and laughing together. We could go on living.

"I find great pleasure in raising my oldest grandson and spending time with the others," Gloria said, smiling. "I have great hopes for their future. On Sundays, they all go to church with me. I refuse to look back. God supplies the strength I need one day at a time."

God's grace had outstripped disappointment, prejudice, and fear. Instead of succumbing to anger and resentment, Gloria chose to love and forgive her children—to a degree she never thought possible. Forgiveness. Some people talk about it. Others, like Gloria, live it.

Love Makes Parents Vulnerable

Connie, Emma, Stuart, Mattie, Gloria, and millions of parents like them make themselves vulnerable because they love their children.

Connie sought Christian counseling after the bedroom confrontation with Rob and his girlfriend. Shortly afterward, in prayer, she was able to release her hurt and forgive her son.

Emma and Stuart, despite many emotional struggles, continue to walk in forgiveness and are still praying their son will be delivered from drugs.

Mattie, in surrendering her expectations of hearing from her son, has developed a deeper trust in the Lord, knowing that He alone can restore the broken relationship.

There's no escaping the risk of being hurt as a parent, but forgiveness is always God's answer.

What Is Forgiveness?

Forgiveness is an act of one's will. It's also a process requiring time to complete, time for one's emotions to come into agreement with the decision one has made. This takes more time for some than for others; but once we decide to take the first step toward forgiveness, we can depend on God's strength to help us continue the process.

As we consider the full meaning of forgiveness, we'll see the following steps as part of the process:
1. Giving up the desire to punish or get even
2. Excusing for a fault or offense
3. Turning from defensiveness
4. Ceasing to feel resentment
5. Renouncing anger
6. Absolving from payment

Consequences of Not Forgiving

Jesus often warned His followers about the consequences of refusing to forgive. He told a story about a servant who owed the king an enormous debt. Millions of dollars. When he begged for mercy, the king had great compassion and wiped away the debt. After he was forgiven, the servant met a man who owed him a very small amount. He demanded that the man pay every cent. When the king heard this, he called the servant, took back his forgiveness, and threw him into jail to be tortured until he could pay back all he owed (see Matthew 18:23–35).

Through this parable, Jesus paints a picture of our relationship to God:
1. God, our King, out of His great compassion, cancels our debts.
2. Like the servant, our sins (debts) against God are so enormous we can never repay them.
3. The sins which others commit against us are small and insignificant compared to our debt to our Master.

4. Our natural bent is to withhold forgiveness.
5. When we refuse to forgive others, we block God's flow of forgiveness to us.[1]

Like the unforgiving servant in Jesus' parable, we suffer torment whenever we refuse to forgive. Anyone who has wrestled with guilt understands this, for guilt is torment. God, through Christ's sacrificial death, has provided an answer to our guilt: He *forgives* us.

Few of us decide intentionally to be unforgiving. So why do we hold on to our anger, bitterness, resentment, and desire for revenge? We fail to forgive because we are fallen human beings, sinners, entangled in a storm of complex emotions.

Since the day Adam and Eve sinned in the Garden of Eden, we have inherited a sinful nature, one driven to self-serving and rebelling against God.

JoAnne Sekowsky summarizes our predicament well:

> While we were lost in our sins and had accumulated this enormous debt, we were in a hopeless situation. We could never pay it off. God had compassion on us. He decided to forgive our debt, but a problem remained. In God's economy, the debt still existed; someone had to pay it for us. God chose to take the responsibility on Himself, and He sent His son, Jesus, to pay it. Obediently, Jesus took our punishment (paid our debt) by dying. He broke the power of our sin nature once and for all. God accepted His Son's sacrifice as sufficient payment for our debt. Now when we accept Jesus as Savior, He marks our account *Paid in Full*.
>
> The only condition God attaches to this transaction is that we keep our account free and clear of charges. Just as we have been forgiven, we, in turn, must forgive anyone who offends us.[2]

That's a strong statement, isn't it? Yet that's God's condition; forgiven by Him, we must forgive those who sin against us. He has not prescribed a legalistic duty; rather He's provided an opportunity to live fully—guilt free!

Release From Debt

The other side of this truth is that, when we choose to forgive, we extend love and mercy to the one forgiven and release him from our judgment. Paul tells us, "Be kind and compassionate to one another, forgiving each other, just as in Christ God forgave you" (Eph. 4:32). In this verse, the word *forgiving* in the original Greek means "to bestow a favor unconditionally." Forgiving, by God's plan, is to *freely bestow favor* on the one who has offended us. Jesus clearly instructed us to: "Forgive and you will be forgiven" (Luke 6:37). Here forgive means to "let loose from," or "to release, set at liberty."[3] When we forgive, we free both ourselves and the one forgiven; our choice gives God the freedom to release both of us.

Forgiveness Assumes Loss

Let me share an experience from our Sunday night church service which gave me a clearer picture of forgiveness.

The service was ending. We were singing a chorus about our owing a debt we could not pay and Jesus paying a debt He did not owe. We sang it over several times. As the closing strain of the chorus faded away, a stranger sitting near the back of the church sprang to his feet and ran to the platform to ask our pastor if he could speak to the congregation.

Taking the microphone, he stammered out his plea: "I want to ask this congregation to forgive me. Some years ago, I robbed your treasurer while he was making a night deposit at the bank. I'm now a Christian, and I ask your forgiveness. I don't have the money to repay you."

A hush settled over our congregation. The pastor quietly took the microphone and spoke slowly and deliberately, "All members of this church who are willing to forgive him say, 'John, I forgive you.'"

All over the sanctuary, voices rose in unison, "John, I forgive you."

The pastor continued, "As I remember, that night's offering was about $500. I'd like to ask all of you men who just forgave John to come forward and pay off John's debt by putting the money in this plate. You see, when we forgive, we assume the loss."

Most of the men didn't know John, a man tormented enough to confess his sin to the whole congregation. Yet a number of them reached into their wallets and went forward to pay off his debt. His obligation was still there. However, when his benefactors paid the debt for him, they assumed the loss. His crime was absolved. His debt cancelled.

Over the years, I've often thought about the pastor's words: "When we forgive, we assume the loss." It's the same when we suffer deep hurts by our children. We assume the loss by forgiving them and refusing to hold a grudge, thus releasing them from the offense. We need to do this repeatedly with both small and large injustices, as forgiveness is not a onetime choice; it's an ongoing process. If we could grasp forgiveness from God's perspective, we would be more willing to freely bestow it on others.

A List of Hurts

A distraught mother, Darla, related an incident that took place the night before she came to a prayer retreat where I was the speaker. Her daughter Cindy thrust a piece of paper into her hand and turned angrily to face her. "Mother, here's a list of things you've done to me since I got married three years ago," she said, flopping down on the sofa. "I decided it was time you knew why I'm so hurt and mad at you and why I don't come to see you more often."

The accusation caught Darla by surprise. Nevertheless she calmly sat down beside Cindy and studied her list of grievances. As she did, a big lump formed in her throat. These things—many of them insignificant to her—had caused her daughter's growing coolness and resentment.

Looking Cindy straight in the eye, Darla said, "Honey, I admit I've said or done everything on your list. But I want you to know I never intended any of these things to hurt you. Can we talk this through so you can forgive me and we can get this hurt healed?"

"Maybe later," Cindy snapped, "I'm going home to cook supper for Joe now." Cindy grabbed her purse and headed for the door. "I just wanted to get this off my chest, Mom, once and for all." She glared at Darla for a moment, then slammed the door.

Sharing her dismay with me that night at the retreat, Darla asked for prayer that her daughter would be open to healing their broken relationship. I prayed with her; then she prayed and asked God's forgiveness for the hurtful words she'd spoken to Cindy. She admitted she felt hurt by Cindy's cutting words and, wisely, identified her own pain by verbally expressing exactly how angry and hurt she'd been. When the rush of emotion subsided, she quietly released her pain and judgments to the Lord and made the choice to forgive her daughter from her heart.

Darla left that retreat confident of a new beginning with her daughter.

Harsh Words Stir Up Anger

Fourteen-year-old Andy was practicing his chords on the piano when his father stuck his head into the living room and said, "Andy, is that all you know?"

To the dad's untrained ear, it sounded as if his son had been playing the same song for hours. Andy immediately stopped playing and never again played the piano for his dad. Years later, in his twenties, Andy confessed to his dad that he'd resented him from that day on, misinterpreting his words to mean his dad didn't accept him or his music.

The budding musician, crushed by his father's words, had harbored his hurt for years. Thankfully, Andy's father, Pastor Charles Stanley of Atlanta, realized there was a wall in their relationship. At his initiation, they patiently worked through their need for forgiveness.[4]

Words or actions can cripple for years. I remember a spanking and tongue-lashing I got on my sixth birthday for something I didn't do. That memory stayed with me until I was grown, but I'm sure my parents had no idea of the wound I nurtured. And so it is with our children. We say or do things out of anger, insensitivity, a wrong reaction, or pride, not realizing that we have emotionally wounded them.

"A harsh word stirs up anger," the writer of Proverbs reminds us. "Pleasant words are a honeycomb, sweet to the soul and healing to the bones" (Prov. 15:1; 16:24).

We can cut our children down when we speak in anger, rebuke, or other thoughtless, emotionally charged ways. Unless forgiveness brings healing, we suffer the consequences of a broken relationship.

How to Forgive: Humble Yourself

God's requirement to restore a broken relationship is simple: "Humble yourself." Not an easy task. Scripture says, "Clothe yourself with humility toward one another, because, 'God opposes the proud but gives grace to the humble.' Humble yourselves, therefore, under God's mighty hand, that he may lift you up in due time" (1 Pet. 5:5,6).

Most of us are afraid to let down our guard in front of our children. What if they see us as we really are? We could risk losing our place of authority in their lives. The fact is, when we ask their forgiveness, we're projecting *true* authority and strength. Such an act of humility on our part can enhance our children's view of us.

When we are wrong, we can simply say, "I shouldn't have said that. You've been hurt by my words. Please forgive me; I'm sorry."

Or we may need to add, "Is there something I can do to help straighten out this misunderstanding?"

Maybe your daughter borrowed your new silk blouse without asking. You can't find it, and when you see her wearing the blouse, you lash out with angry words and create a big scene.

"I'm sorry I flew off the handle," you could say. "I was angry when I saw you wearing my blouse without asking. I know my words were harsh. Will you forgive me?"

Genuine humility will often encourage the child to ask your forgiveness for his or her behavior, and you can then discuss the entire episode without inflammatory, hurtful words.

One transparent mother of five told me, "When you see your own flesh—sons and daughters—do something you've fought in yourself all your life and discover it growing before you in your kids, you know we're all sinners, that nobody is good but God. My oldest daughter did all the things 'good girls' don't do, but, if I had had the courage as a youngster, I probably would have done the same things. How could I *not* forgive my children?"

Keeping Promises

One of the primary ways parents offend their children is by failing to keep their promises. Have you ever promised a child something without taking it seriously, then just forgot? One mom who shared with me was big enough to apologize.

"Liz, I failed you," she told her daughter. "I promised I'd take off from work and drive you to Atlanta to the art festival. But I got busy and didn't ask for time off until it was too late. I'm sorry I let you down; please forgive me, dear."

The mother's willingness to apologize and ask her daughter's forgiveness prevented a long build-up of resentment and the relationship was quickly restored.

Usually we give every possible excuse to our children, rather than honestly confess, "I'm sorry—I blew it. I made a promise, but I failed to carry out my word." Of course, there are times when our children fail to keep their word, too. We need to be charitable toward them at those times.

When we fail to do what we agreed to do, the problem usually is that our priorities are out of line. Instead of apologizing and asking our kids to forgive us, we offer an excuse. "My boss wanted us to go out. We couldn't say no, even though we told you we'd come and see you in your school play. That's the way life is; you've just got to grow up and accept it."

The child walks away thinking he's not valuable or important to the family—that Dad's boss is more significant than he is.

We defeat our purpose when we approach reconciliation with a judgmental, self-righteous attitude. Instead, we need to be non-accusing, gentle, humble. We can begin by asking our child what promises we have made that we haven't fulfilled. If possible, we must fulfill them. If impossible, we can only ask forgiveness and release from the promises we cannot keep.

Right Timing and Right Attitude

When we know our words or actions have hurt our children, we need to do something about it as soon as the opportunity seems right. However, it's crucial to pray for the right timing, the right words, and the right motive and attitude for ourselves and our child. Here is a suggested model for such a prayer:

"Father, I ask you to prepare my child to receive my words of apology. Help me speak honestly from my heart. Lord, I trust you to prepare the way and create the opportunity for this ministry of forgiveness to take place. Thank you, Lord, that you will

give victory in this situation and the enemy will have no part in our conversation. Thank you for your forgiveness, in Jesus' name, Amen."

Choosing the right time and atmosphere is essential. We shouldn't keep a child up late on a school night for a heart-to-heart talk, nor should we approach him when he's in his room talking with his friends. However, we should not procrastinate on such an important matter. Pray for God's perfect timing.

Avoid Offending Again

After we've asked forgiveness, we need to avoid committing the same offenses again. If my son tells me I don't listen to him when he talks, I need to work hard at paying attention. This is a good reminder to most parents: We should pay close attention when we speak with our children, so we won't half-heartedly promise something we can't later fulfill.

In an experience with my son, I learned that my words have to be backed up with action. I once criticized him for allowing others to take advantage of his graphic arts talent without paying him for his work. He was free-lancing from our home and trying to save money for Bible college.

"Mom, don't get involved with my financial affairs!" he fired back at me.

"I'm sorry," I said, "but I hate to see you work so long and hard and not get paid. The Bible says that the laborer is worthy of his pay. But I'll try to keep quiet."

"Saying you're sorry isn't enough," he said emphatically. "How about repentance? That means you'll stop doing it." He was right. Repentance is a change of attitude, making a decision not to do it again. I made that decision that day.

"The grandest expression of love is to forgive," says Christian psychologist Richard P. Walters. "It is our most unselfish act and therefore the most difficult and rewarding." [5]

Our act of forgiveness, like Jesus' act of love on the cross, will have a profound impact on the child we forgive. We make the choice.

Once you recognize your need to forgive, these guidelines will help you follow through:

1. Choose to forgive by an act of your will; it is a decision, not an emotion.
2. Ask God for His supernatural ability to love and forgive; ask Him to love that person through you according to Romans 5:5.
3. Thank the Lord for all He has forgiven you.
4. Thank God for the blessings you've received from the person you need to forgive. (Ask Him to reveal them to you if you have difficulty with this step.)
5. Recognize that the person who hurt you probably had deep needs in his or her life.
6. Pray God's blessings upon that person's life; bless him or her with your words—do not curse.
7. Recognize that forgiving this person is a condition for you to continue receiving God's forgiveness in your own life (Matt. 6:14,15).

It is critically important to remember that forgiveness is a progressive thing, a way of life we need to nurture. Many hurts and resentments have been buried for years, and we need to *allow time* for the Holy Spirit to change and renew our thoughts once we have opened ourselves to the forgiveness process. As the fruit of the Spirit is cultivated in our lives (Gal. 5:22,23), forgiving offenses becomes easier, because we have a strong desire to please our heavenly Father and to "keep in step with the Spirit" (Gal. 5:25).

Remember the proverb that says, "Humility comes before honor" (Prov. 15:33)? If we humble ourselves, God will honor us. Even if our children don't forgive us, God will, when we have the right motive and desire to stop offending our children by our words and our actions.

Prayer

Thank You, Father, for sending Jesus as an atonement for my sins. Thank You for forgiving me and enabling me to forgive those who wrong me. Help me to be willing to continually forgive my children—and all others who hurt me.

Lord, help me speak pleasant, encouraging words to my children; help me to bless them and not to curse them through careless words. Show me how to humble myself and make amends. I ask in Jesus' name, Amen.

TWO

Accepting Forgiveness

Christian parents who cannot or will not forgive themselves will struggle to forgive their children. When we refuse to forgive ourselves, we are saying, "Jesus' sacrifice is not sufficient for me."

Take Claudia, for example, a mother who wrestled with her own sense of failure. "I've told the Lord dozens of times that I've forgiven my son for robbing a convenience store and going to prison," she told me through her tears as I was praying with her after a ladies' meeting. "But the ugly words I shouted at Bob when I was mad—words like 'stupid' and 'disgraceful'—still ring in my ears night and day."

Claudia had written Bob in prison and asked his forgiveness; and he'd written back, assuring her he wanted their relationship restored. Still, she had no peace.

"Honey, if you and Bob have forgiven each other, then God forgives you both," I assured her. "Just accept His forgiveness. You see, the enemy wants to torment you with guilt; but you must believe what God says, not what the enemy says. Believe the truth." For her that was the enabling key. After we talked, she prayed again, accepted God's gift of forgiveness, and left with a gleam of victory in her eye.

"The Ding-Dong Principle"

I told Claudia a story about the renowned Dutch evangelist, Corrie Ten Boom, which has helped me whenever I struggle with self-condemnation. Miss Ten Boom, who became a "tramp for the Lord" following her release from a German concentration camp, was speaking in Europe. A young woman came up after one meeting for prayer.

Corrie directed her attention to the church bell.

"Up in that church tower is a bell which is rung by pulling on a rope," she said. "After the sexton lets go of the rope, the bell keeps on swinging. First ding, then dong. Slower and slower until there's a final dong and it stops. When we forgive someone, we take our hands off the rope. But if we've been tugging at our grievances for a long time, we mustn't be surprised when the old angry thoughts keep coming for awhile. They're just the ding-dongs of the old bell slowing down." [1]

Though God forgets, we humans remember our old sins. These are the ding-dongs of our past life. How badly we need to stop "preserving the evidence" in our memory banks and focus on God's promise to forgive us:

"If we confess our sins, He is faithful and righteous to forgive us our sins and to cleanse us from all unrighteousness" (1 John 1:9 NASB).

I Had an Abortion Last Night

After the first session of a women's retreat I was leading in South Carolina, Rose, a large women in her thirties came forward.

Holding her head down and shuffling along, she was a classic picture of despair. "I need prayer," she mumbled.

"What for?" I asked, looking up into her face as she towered over me.

"I had an abortion last night," she whispered, staring at the floor. "Can God forgive me? Can I forgive myself?" she asked, searching my face with pain-filled eyes.

I began praying with her. Others gathered around to offer love and support to this hurting woman. Later that evening, after much prayer and counseling, Rose worked through to a big "Yes!" answer to both her questions. She accepted Jesus as Lord of her life for the first time. She "let go of the rope," received God's unfailing forgiveness, and forgave herself.

I hardly recognized Rose at the morning session the next day. Walking erect, with her shoulders no longer stooped, she didn't hesitate to look me straight in the eye with a broad smile. She went home from the retreat a transformed person.

God's Way of Forgiveness

Episcopal priest Everett Fullam wrote that Scripture refers to God's forgiveness in at least three ways:

1. He takes our sins and casts them behind His back (Isa. 38:17). He puts our sins out of His sight.
2. He separates our sins from us as far as the east is from the west. In other words, He puts our sins out of His reach (Psa. 103:12).
3. When He forgives our sins, He remembers them no more. He puts our sins out of His mind (Jer. 31:34). [2]

God's way of forgiveness—forgetting our sins—is far superior to our holding on, remembering, and rehashing them.

Accept His Gift

God's forgiveness is a free gift, yet thousands of Christians have not yet accepted this special gift for themselves.

Alma confessed to me that she was one. It began when her younger daughter Renee decided to have her wedding in her fiance's home town, too far away for her own family and friends to attend. To make matters worse, she greatly overestimated the number of guests, causing thousands of dollars of needless expense, not to mention all the left-over wedding cake and refreshments. After the wedding, when Renee showed an utter lack of gratitude for her parents' help, Alma's irritation mushroomed into bitterness.

One morning as Alma was complaining to the Lord about Renee's attitude, she sensed His response: "All these years, you asked Me to give your daughter a husband who loved Me. Didn't I do that?"

"Oh, Lord, I'm sorry; forgive me," she cried. "Yes, having Renee marry a Christian husband is far more important than the wedding extravagance. . .or that my family and friends were unable to attend. . .or even my daughter's ingratitude. I confess my resentment, Lord, and I forgive her."

Alma had forgiven her daughter, but she had not yet appropriated God's forgiveness for her own self-incrimination. "Can God forgive me? As a Christian, I should have known better than to let unforgiveness creep over me like a dark cloud," she lamented.

Alma, however, was determined. She went back to the Lord, spilled out her feelings of failure, and chose to receive forgiveness for herself. Then God dropped a wonderful idea into her mind: Why not fly those long miles to become reconciled and reacquainted with her married daughter?

Just before leaving, Alma called me. I could hear genuine openness in her voice. "My daughter is excited that I'm coming and is taking a week off from work to be with me. I am ready to see her now that I've forgiven her and received God's forgiveness for my own part as well. If God leads me to talk about the forgiveness issue, I'm willing; I'll just wait for His timing. But I know for certain He's changed my heart toward Renee."

This mother experienced first-hand what God promises in His

Word: "I have swept away your offenses like a cloud, your sins like the morning mist" (Isa. 44:22).

Should Alma bring up past hurts while visiting her daughter, she should not assume Renee will forgive her. Offering to forgive a child who has hurt us is not contingent upon her being willing to forgive us. Forgiveness, like love, is a risk. Yet in faith and by our choice, we offer it whether the child forgives us or not. That's a risk God asks us to take.

When Tragedy Strikes

Losing a child in an accident presents an especially difficult challenge for parents. It's so easy to assign blame—to ourselves or others. Many have learned the hard way that blaming only pulls us into a downward spiral of bitterness and anger; it is always a dead-end street.

Marie, the mother of three young children ages four to eight, left them with her husband while she went to a nearby town to help a friend through an emergency. David, who willingly agreed to keep the children, decided to take them to some family property where he and his brother were clearing trees to create a pasture.

The children played while the men worked, but soon an argument broke out between the two boys—Carl, the eight-year-old, and Sandy, the six-year-old. Finally, David separated them, making Sandy sit on the hood of his uncle's pick-up truck. Carl and Anita sat on their own truck until the work was finished.

As the men were felling the last tree that day, the chain saw jammed. David wedged a piece of wood in to free the saw, not realizing it would make the tree fall in the wrong direction.

Seconds later, the tree fell across the hood of the truck, striking Sandy and severely crushing his head. He died before they reached the hospital.

A family member called Marie with the news, and she rushed home.

Because Sandy had been so badly mangled in the accident, David convinced Marie not to view his body.

"After he was buried, I resented the fact that David had made that decision for me," she told me. "I felt unfairly denied a final goodbye to my son."

In the ensuing months, Marie let anger, bitterness and unforgiveness devour her. Nothing was the same anymore. "I blamed myself for 'being there' for a friend, but not for my own children.

"I regretted not being able to comfort Carl and Anita, who witnessed the accident. I regretted not being there to hold and comfort Sandy on the way to the hospital—to say 'Goodbye' and 'I love you' one last time.

"I was angry at my husband for his carelessness when our children's lives were at stake, while doing work he knew could be dangerous. Each time I heard him blame himself, I was convinced more and more that it was his fault."

She was also angry with Carl, who picked on his younger brother and caused him to be on that truck when the tree fell. She remembered that several days before the accident Sandy had run into the house crying, "Mommy, Carl doesn't love me anymore." Now those words replayed in her mind like a broken record. Every time she looked at Carl, she almost exploded with anger.

Blaming God

Most of all, Marie blamed God.

"I had always believed that God never slumbers nor sleeps, but now He had let me down. I began thinking of Him as wide awake, but uncaring. I had almost miscarried before Sandy was born. It seemed a cruel trick that God allowed him to be born, only to snatch him away again after I'd invested six years of love in him.

"I felt cheated by God and His Word. I didn't want to pray, and I didn't enjoy going to church. When I was around our friends, it seemed unfair that their children were safe and healthy and my son was dead." Marie wiped copious tears as she told her story.

Bitterness ate at her heart like acid, and she became physically ill. Her heart felt like a lead weight in her body. Breathing was difficult. As grief consumed her, she began thinking she, too, might die.

Even in her downward slide, she became conscious of David's picking up her bitterness toward God and how their bitterness was affecting her children. She saw what she was doing—lashing out at God and missing the comfort only He could give her.

Tired of all the debilitating emotions, Marie fell into her worn armchair and began releasing her feelings: "Oh, God, I was so unfair to accuse you of indifference in letting my precious son be killed. You know what it is like to lose a son—Your only Son. How could I have been so wrong?" Repentant, she wept and prayed for a long time. Finally able to say the words, "Please forgive me," Marie opened herself to receive the cleansing power of Jesus.

"However, it was not until several months later, at a retreat, that a deeper healing took place in my life," Marie told me. "I forgave my husband, my son Carl, and myself once and for all. None of us can be blamed for Sandy's death. Oh yes, I forgave God, too! Amazingly, I have regained strength to go on living; all my physical symptoms are gone."

A Stronger, Closer Family

Unforgiveness, Marie discovered, is a lot like a polio virus: contagious and crippling. Filled with her own grief and anger, she became blind to her husband's and son's struggles. As she worked her way to forgiveness, they followed her example.

Carl required more time in the healing process, as he harbored deep guilt over starting the quarrel with Sandy. Fortunately, a Christian couple was able to help him accept God's unconditional forgiveness. In the end, the entire family received emotional healing.

Marie is grateful Carl's life was spared and that he is developing into an outgoing, warm, and loving young man. She's forgiven him for any fault she ever accused him of.

"I love him because he is my son—valuable and dear," she said, "I thank God for every day we had as a family before Sandy's death. Although we're a changed, different family now, we're also a stronger, closer family. I know the joy of restored fellowship with God since accepting His forgiveness."

Praise God! As Corrie ten Boom often said, "Saints, take your hands off the rope—let go. Let God."

Prayer

Lord, forgive me for not believing the blood of Jesus is sufficent to cover my sins. I accept Your forgiveness, and I choose to forgive myself. I refuse to listen to the lies of the accuser any longer. Heavenly Father, I believe Your Word that says my offenses are wiped away like a heavy mist, buried in the sea of forgetfulness, forgiven, and forgotten by You. Thank You for such reassurance. I praise You for allowing Jesus to die for me. What an all-sufficent, all-encompassing Father You are to me! In Jesus' name, Amen.

Three

Forgiving Your Parents

Somewhere in life, most of us discover, perhaps traumatically, that our parents are human, with faults and weaknesses like everyone else. They aren't the perfect parents we wanted them to be. As a result, we experienced hurts in our childhood—perhaps through thoughtless words spoken in anger, through neglect, even abuse or incest. No matter what the hurts were, we need to forgive them.

Since we reap what we sow, I believe when we forgive our parents, it frees our children to forgive us, too.

I Closed My Heart

All night long the wheels of the train echoed the dreary song in my aching heart as I sobbed myself to sleep in the berth below my mother and six-year-old sister. *Anger. Hurt. Betrayal.*

All I could think about was lashing out to hurt the one who was hurting me—my daddy. Poisonous thoughts shot through my mind

35

like invisible darts. *How dare he do this to us? What kind of a father would ship his own family away on a train?*

Daddy had driven us to the New Orleans train station to send us to my aunt's in Florida. I was twelve at the time and far too timid to tell him how angry and hurt I was at him for sending us away—especially at Christmastime—and for making me leave behind my two brothers, all my friends, and our comfortable brick home. Unable to express my feelings, I simply closed my heart to him and silently vowed, "I'll never forgive him."

The Ugly Word

That morning as he put us on the train, I overheard a whisper of the ugly word—*divorce*. The next summer, that word became reality; Daddy married his secretary. By then, Mother had custody of my brothers, so in a sense we were "family" once more.

We lived in northwest Florida, where Mother worked long hours managing a small old hotel her sister owned. After five years of hard work, she saved enough to make a down payment on an old clapboard boarding house in Tallahassee, where she could help her four children get their education. At the time, I was too immature to appreciate her foresight. Remembering the comfortable home we'd left behind, I was ashamed of the peeling paint and sagging front porch of this place we now called home.

Mother often put in fourteen-hour days of backbreaking labor taking care of forty boarders in this shabby old southern house standing in the shadow of the gleaming white state capitol building.

When I heard her in the kitchen at five o'clock in the morning preparing breakfast, feelings of anger and resentment toward Daddy often returned. I relived the painful separation over again in my mind.

Besides cooking for our boarders, Mother daily served more than three hundred people family-style meals in shifts in our dining room. My sister and I helped her, serving tables for college kids, construction workers, legislators, and state office workers. Our job also included sitting at the desk in the lobby to collect the fifty cents charged for each meal. We were glad we could help Mother that much, but the bulk of the work fell on her shoulders. She never complained or displayed any bitterness toward my father.

As the years passed, Mother's hair turned gray; her legs dragged with arthritic pain; and my bitterness toward Daddy grew. Although I was a Christian and attended church regularly, I took no responsibility for my ugly attitude. I continued to blame Daddy for Mother's having to work so hard, and justified the resentment growing within me.

Do You Have Anything Against Anyone?

One day in my late thirties with three children of my own, something startling happened which became the turning point of my whole life. While visiting Mother in a little Florida fishing village where she had retired, I went along to a Thursday night service at the Episcopal church she attended.

The music was lively and happy, but it was the people who astounded me. They looked so joyful standing with upraised arms and glowing faces, singing with all their hearts as they worshiped God.

It was beautiful—like nothing I'd ever seen—and I realized these people were demonstrating a depth of Christian faith I desperately needed. I made an appointment with the minister, the Reverend Forrest Mobley. The next week he explained what I'd seen that night.

"Those folks not only know Jesus as Savior and Lord," he said, "but they've asked the Holy Spirit to fill their lives. It all starts with repentance."

Then he asked me a pointed question: "Do you have anything against anyone?"

His words hit me like a thunderbolt! Instantly, I thought of Daddy. I knew Jesus had taught us to pray, "Forgive us our trespasses as we forgive those who trespass against us." After all those years of pent-up resentment and bitterness, could I forgive Daddy? Speechless, I hung my head, pondering the question.

"It's my dad," I said haltingly. "I don't know whether I can forgive him or not, but I'm willing for God to make me willing to forgive."

"That's not scriptural," Father Mobley replied, gently shaking his head. "You must *choose* to forgive—not wait until you 'feel willing.' You say it, and God will do it."

I became defensive, telling him I had a right to be bitter because of the terrible thing Daddy had done.

"Your father is responsible for his own wrong-doing," he explained. "You must release your anger and ask forgiveness for your wrong attitude if you want to receive God's peace and blessing."

I Made the Choice

I struggled, but finally made the choice to forgive.

"Good. Now pray aloud so it will have meaning for you," the pastor continued. "I'll agree with you in prayer and be a witness to your confession."

He asked me to kneel at the coffee table in his office. I'd never knelt in my church except when I was installed as an officer, and I felt awkward—yet, at the same time, willing. "God, I forgive Daddy," I prayed, lifting my open palms ever so slightly as though pushing this burden right into my heavenly Father's lap.

Then, reluctantly, I added, "Lord, forgive me for hating him."

Immediately waves of deep, deep love pulsated through me as my tears spilled onto the red carpet. It seemed to lift my whole body; I even felt it tingling in my toes. But the best part of all was that, as I closed my eyes, I could almost picture my daddy walking with Jesus, talking with Him. A Bible verse I'd read sometime earlier came to mind again as a promise just for me:

"He will restore the hearts of the fathers to their children, and the hearts of the children to their fathers" (Mal. 4:6 NASB).

Father Mobley prayed that Jesus would live through me and fill me to overflowing with the Holy Spirit. The warmth of His presence seemed to envelop me. When I opened my eyes and saw the red carpet all around me, I realized the truth of being immersed in the blood of Jesus and cleansed of my sin of unforgiveness. Jesus was now *Lord* of my life, and I felt I loved everyone in the whole world.

"Dear Daddy. . ."

Some weeks later, I felt an urgency to write to my dad. I was experiencing such freedom from my longstanding anger that I was eager to have our relationship restored. Perhaps with more zeal than wisdom, I sent him a Bible, then some books that had helped me in my new Christian walk.

Daddy wrote back saying he enjoyed the new Bible translation I'd sent. In fact, he said he'd read it through in a few months. He found some of the other books interesting, he said, but he didn't agree with one. He wrote me a letter detailing its faults.

Unfortunately, I personalized his remarks, feeling rejected along with the book. Yet I was determined to remain open to him and not allow the old bitterness to steal my newfound peace. I kept writing him about how my life was changing, praying that Jesus would restore our relationship regardless of this new hurt. He always answered my letters and said he enjoyed the Christian magazines I sent him.

Catching Up on Life

One day five years later, Daddy called to say he was coming to visit us. At the end of that week, I drove to my sister's house to pick him up. When I got out of the car, he was standing in her back yard tossing a ball to her small son. Our eyes met; I smiled and walked to where he stood. "Hello, Dad," I said, draping a limp arm across his bony, stooped shoulders. "I'm glad you're here." All I could manage was a touch, but that was a big step.

I was still fighting frustration. Yes, I'd forgiven him; my heart told me I no longer hated him. But we were strangers. Hugging wouldn't have been appropriate.

"God, help me," I prayed silently as I drove him to my house. "Help me get to know this man."

On our screened porch the next night, I began drawing him out in conversation. "Dad," I coaxed, "Tell me about your childhood. I want to know what your growing up days were like." He laughed and leaned far back in his chair, staring at the stars. I couldn't remember ever hearing him laugh before.

The next two days were filled with catching up on life that had passed us by. He rode along in the car when I took a son to the beach and a daughter to the eye doctor. Then we went shopping for clothes. Too soon, it was time for him to leave. As he got into the car for me to drive him to the bus station, he began to talk about our relationship.

Forgiven! Forgiven! Forgiven!

"How could you love me?" he asked, his voice breaking with emotion. "After all I've done...after all..." He couldn't continue.

I was unable to speak, too choked up to tell him about the hate I'd turned over to Jesus. But I think he knew. After three days of being with us, eating with us, joining us for family devotions, I think he knew. I loved him because I'd forgiven him. And because I'd forgiven him, God had forgiven me of all my bitterness, resentment, hate, and faultfinding. How wonderful to be free from the weight of that load.

I reached across the front seat and hugged him, holding him tightly for a moment like a child clutching a treasured teddy bear.

"It's all right, Daddy," I whispered.

He took a deep breath and seemed relieved that that painful chapter of our lives was behind us. We drove to the station in silence.

After seeing him safely on the bus, I thought of that scene more than twenty years earlier when he had put me on the train. "Thank you, Lord," I said, smiling up at the sky. "You do good work!"

As the bus pulled away and picked up momentum, the hum of the tires seemed to echo the thoughts swirling through my mind. *"Forgiven, Forgiven, Forgiven."* The song had changed.

He Forgave Mom, Too

When my husband completed twenty years as an engineer for the government, he took early retirement from NASA, Kennedy Space Center. We moved to the little fishing village where Mom lived and took care of her during her long bout with cancer. Just before her seventy-second birthday, she went to be with the Lord. Soon afterwards Dad came to spend a day with me, and I drove him past the cemetery where Mom was buried.

"I prayed for her every day because she sacrificed her life for you children," Dad said thoughtfully.

I assured him she had forgiven him, and he assured me he had forgiven her, too. As we talked that day, I felt the peaceful confidence that he and Mom would spend eternity with Jesus.

Forgiving My Stepmother

My hardest struggle was to forgive my stepmother; I had always blamed her for breaking up our home. From my childhood perspective, I could only see her as the intruder. But on my way to a speaking engagement one winter, I drove out of my way to visit Daddy and her just for an hour. As I approached their house, a truck sped around me, slingling red clay onto my car's windshield.

During our brief visit, I mentioned to Daddy that I couldn't leave before cleaning my windshield.

While we talked, his wife took a sponge and pan of water and wiped away the red mud—just as God had wiped the ugly, unwanted mud from my heart. I hugged her and she hugged back. At last, I realized I'd forgiven her. Resentment was gone, and joy filled my heart.

Consider Jesus' words when He said, "Forgive, and you will be forgiven" (Luke 6:37). The original Greek word for *forgive* in this verse means "to fully relieve, release, dismiss, pardon, let go, loose, set at liberty." [1] That's exactly what I had done. I had released, let go, pardoned my dad and his wife; and they were now free. In turn, I also was released, set free, and pardoned by the Lord Jesus.

I believe that recognizing my earthly father's weaknesses has helped me recognize my own flaws more clearly. As a result, it's been easier to forgive my own children.

Sowing and Reaping

If we allow bitterness, anger, and resentment to linger in our thoughts, it can sicken our minds and spirits and even negatively affect our physical health.

A bitter, stoop-shouldered, eighty-year-old woman suffering with cancer once told me, "I'll never forgive Papa. He made me work in the cotton mill and give him my paycheck every month. I wanted to save it to go to college. I got my college education piecemeal years later by waiting tables in the dorm and cleaning homes for the rich. Papa never let me date. When I finally married, it was too late in life to have children. Papa—he sure wasn't much of a loving papa."

And sadly, the woman wasn't much of a forgiving daughter. The apostle Paul teaches clearly the law of sowing and reaping:

> "Do not be deceived: God cannot be mocked. A man reaps what he sows. The one who sows to please his sinful nature [*unforgiveness*], from that nature will

reap destruction; the one who sows to please the Spirit [*forgiveness*], from the Spirit will reap eternal life. Let us not become weary in doing good, for at the proper time we will reap a harvest if we do not give up" (Gal. 6:7–9, bracketed notes added).

I personally believe that when we forgive our parents—no matter how grievous our hurts—it frees our children to forgive us.

Honor Your Father and Mother

Though our parents may have hurt us in ways that are terribly wrong, we cannot dismiss the biblical command: "Children... 'Honor your father and mother'—which is the first commandment with a promise—'that it may go well with you and that you may enjoy long life on the earth' " (Eph. 6:2).

"To honor" means "to prize, to revere, value." [2] This is the fifth commandment, and it is the only commandment that carries a promise.

How can we value, revere, honor, and forgive a parent who has deeply and perhaps deliberately hurt us? Let's face it, many mothers and fathers have not earned the right to be honored. Some have deserted their children, abused their children, ignored their children, and browbeaten their children. However, until we see them as flawed people, people whom Christ can redeem, we will not have the compassion necessary to release them from our judgments. And, in a real sense, we negate the power of the blood of Jesus to cleanse *all sin*.

Forgiving Incest

Of the known sexual abuse of children in our country, 75 percent is committed by one of the child's own parents. The victims are usually girls between eight and twelve years of age, with 20 percent under seven. [3]

One girl out of four and one boy out of ten will be sexually assaulted at least once by the age of eighteen. For those trapped in the web of incest, the average period of abuse is seven years. [4]

Often when I've prayed for hurting women at Christian gatherings, several will come forward who've never before told anyone about suffering incest. I asked one woman, the third generation in her family to suffer sexual abuse, why she waited so long to deal with this hurt. Her answer wrenched my heart: "Because of all the *guilt, fear, and shame* I felt."

Another woman, whose nightmare of incest lasted nine years, writes, "Shame and fear work together to keep a strangle-hold on a child's ability to call out for help. The fear of losing daddy's love, breaking up the family, or telling and not being believed is enough to keep most children quiet." [5]

Long after the physical abuse ended, this woman had severe emotional scars. Her road to healing began at age twenty-one when she opened her heart to Jesus, admitted her true feelings, and asked God to help her deal with them.

Incest is undoubtedly the most painful injustice many women ever encounter. Yet, as this woman and other victims know, healing is possible. The following guidelines have proven helpful for the road to recovery:

1. Recognize you are not responsible for the wrong choices of others. You would never have initiated those encounters. Ask God to release you from any *false guilt* you may have.
2. You are not the one to suffer *shame*. The sin was not in your heart. Someone you trusted mistreated you by his own wrong choice. Ask God to remove the shame you felt—the frightening, painful experience of feeling dirty and worthless.
3. To rid yourself of *fear*, ask God to replace fear with power, love, and a sound mind (2 Tim. 1:7 KJV). Talk to the Lord about it honestly. Ask Him to remove the fear.
4. If you blame God for allowing you to be abused, forgive Him. He gave mankind freedom of choice and He ran the

risk of people using that freedom to hurt others. God so loved us He sent His only son to die. Jesus knows what it is like to suffer innocently. He can relate to your pain and can comfort you in your sorrow.

5. Forgive your abuser. You will need to admit and own the feelings you have toward that person. No freedom is possible until you forgive the one who sinned against you.

6. Ask God to forgive you of the bitterness, hate, and rebellion you have allowed to fill your life as a result of your molestation. Ask Him to forgive you if you have let it affect your relationships with other people (your husband, father, son, other men).

Accept God's forgiveness, remembering that this is a process. Tell Him out loud that you accept it and continue to affirm your choice if doubts return to plague you.

"God, Bless My Father"

A minister's wife tells of her struggle to forgive her father for her sexual abuse nightmare which began when she was thirteen. After suffering mistreatment for two years, Deborah told her mother, who was devastated by the revelation. Her father eventually left home with another woman.

After she grew up, became a Christian, and married, Deborah continued struggling with unforgiveness toward her dad. "My problem was that I knew I should forgive my father. I was aware that Jesus said, 'If you do not forgive men their sins, your Father will not forgive your sins.' I began to understand that the reason God wants us to forgive is so that we can be like Him. He wants us, His children, to have the same character He has."

One specific verse became ammunition for Deborah's spiritual battle with unforgiveness: "[Love] takes no account of the evil done to it—pays no attention to a suffered wrong" (1 Cor. 13:5 TAB).

Every day, she meditated on God's love and read Bible passages about deliverance and forgiveness, memorizing some of them. Not only did she renew her mind; in the process, she prayed positively for her dad, for she longed to see him come to the Lord.

"God, bless my father," she prayed. "If he'd had his mind trained on You, he would never have done what he did to me. I do not hold him responsible. Bring him into a right, godly state of mind. I forgive him."

One day her father asked her point blank, "Deborah, do you really forgive me?"

A moment of truth. Looking deep into his eyes, she remembered all the years she'd struggled to replace her hurt with God's love. But God had been at work. She could say from her heart, "I forgive you, Dad." That evening her father received Jesus as Lord of his life.

Any of us needing to forgive an abusive parent can look to Deborah's actions as a sound pattern to follow: Begin to meditate on the Scriptures and pray for the parent's salvation and deliverance. Most of us have no idea what happened in our parents' background that may have driven them to such destructive behavior. More than likely, they experienced abuse as well.

Often the child needs to forgive not only the father who was the abuser, but also the mother or other relatives who might have known of the assaults but did nothing to stop them. For some incest victims, forgiving a passive or fearful "bystander" (often the mother) who did nothing to protect him or her is more difficult than forgiving the abusive father.

Look For Good Qualities

For some who have been deeply injured by their parents, the forgiveness process can be helped along by acknowledging any good qualities the parents had.

Shawn, a college student living with his mother and aunt in a low-cost housing project, had never known his father. His mother gave him a bitter and ugly image of the man who had gotten her pregnant. Once his father came to see him, but his mother wouldn't let Shawn out the screen door to meet him.

The boy grew up gifted with musical ability that earned him a college scholarship. He became organist and choir director for his church. Years passed before he understood that, as a Christian, he had to forgive his father for not providing life's needs or emotional support.

"I can't keep carrying Mom's personal grudge against my father," he told the Lord. "Help me forgive and honor my dad. Forgive me and forgive both of them."

Not long afterwards, he realized his father must have some good qualities—perhaps his musical talent and outgoing personality was inherited from his dad. He no longer saw his dad as a totally cruel villain, but simply as a man who made a mistake. Then he was able to forgive his mother for trying to turn Shawn against him.

Forgive, Then Honor

God commands us to honor our parents, whether or not we think our parents deserve it. We are an inseparable part of them, and they are an inseparable part of us. Family counselors Gary Smalley and John Trent explain:

> "We pick up many (of our parents') emotional characteristics and bents, and our physical bodies are forever marked by them, too. Chromosomes are God's building blocks for our physical development, and at conception, half of them came from each parent. From that one fact alone, it should be obvious that we can never escape our parents. Each of our cells bears the vestiges of their stamp on our lives. . .When God tells us to honor our parents, it's with good reason. When

we lower their value and cut them down, we're dishonoring a part of ourselves." [6]

Often we will have to set our wills and *decide* to forgive our parents and to honor them. But this dual decision—first to forgive, then to honor—releases them and frees us to receive God's promise of a long life.

Prayer

Lord, I forgive my parents for all the things they did and the words they spoke that hurt me and wounded my spirit. Some are so deeply buried that I haven't admitted them to anyone; I ask You to heal these hurts. I choose to release my parents and set them free from any judgment I have held them in through my unforgiveness. Lord, not only do I forgive them, but I ask You to forgive them, too. Father, please restore our broken relationship. Forgive me for the things I've said or thought against them that were not honoring to them or pleasing to You. I repent. Thank You for these two who gave me birth. Lord, I receive Your forgiveness. Thank You for the cleansing that it brings. Thank You that, when I forgive, You forgive me, too. In Jesus' name I pray, Amen.

Four

Parents' Right Response

"Wait until that kid gets home! I'll tear him up," the enraged father shouted as he paced the den floor at three in the morning. "If I lose any more sleep, I won't get to work on time. It's not unreasonable to expect a sixteen-year-old to be in at midnight!"

"But what if something awful has happened to him, like a car wreck?" his wife sobbed as she poured the last of the coffee. "You've got to have mercy, Daniel, and consider why Ted is over three hours late coming home. . ."

Can you identify with this angry father and worried mom? Have you ever vacillated between anger and anxiety because your child wasn't home by curfew? As a mother who had three in their teens at the same time, I can relate. Sometimes I was convinced my children never knew that Alexander Graham Bell had invented the telephone.

Why do so many of us fail in handling everyday situations with our children? I see at least two reasons: (1) We tend to react out of our own suspicions and hurts. (2) We seldom ask the Lord for wisdom to handle our reactions or the child's discipline following an infraction of household rules.

The Meaning of Grace

My former pastor, Peter Lord, shared an interesting example of the way God inspired him to wisely avoid a wrong reaction when John, his youngest son, reached teenage years.

At eleven one night, Pastor Lord discovered that John had crawled out the window of his room and left. "I was angry and tired. This was inconvenient, to say the least," he reported. "I was also afraid of what might happen to him.

"It is at times like these that a parent needs to hear from God," he added. *"An inappropriate reaction by a parent to a child's misbehavior is just as wrong as the child's behavior and perhaps more destructive."*

It took Pastor Lord nearly two hours to get quiet enough to hear from the Lord while waiting for John to come home. But the instructions God gave him were quite startling. "Don't discipline him tonight. Wait until tomorrow when you have a clear head."

The next morning, he asked the Lord what to do. Again, the answer surprised him. "Give John a full pardon without punishment, and then explain to him the meaning of grace." [1]

Needless to say, John was relieved.

John didn't deserve his father's grace. He was "let off the hook" instead of being punished because Pastor Lord absolved him of guilt. The word *grace* means "benefit, favor, or gift." When we repent, God does not deal with us according to our sins, but He blesses us with His grace—the gift of undeserved favor—and He absolves us of guilt (See Psalm 103:10; Ephesians 2:8,9).

I Know She Can Do Better

Parents' expectations for their child's academic achievement affect the way they react at report-card time. Recently, when my husband was in the hospital I asked his nurse about her family.

"My daughter brought home a C on her report card last night, so I've decided not to have a birthday party for her this weekend when she turns eight," she related.

"Is that really fair?" I asked, watching her adjust the IV tube. "Do you want her to always remember that Mom cancelled her eighth birthday party because of a math grade? Can't you find some other way to discipline or to help her improve? I still remember punishment I received on my birthday as a child and how wounded I was."

"I never thought about my reaction as wounding her," she replied, looking surprised. "I only thought about my own disappointment, because I know she can do better in math."

"If you don't mind my saying so, I think you may need to forgive your little girl for disappointing you," I said carefully. "You could set her free by forgiving her."

"Really!" she exclaimed, looking at me intently. I had obviously gotten her attention. She quietly gathered up her equipment to leave the room, thinking over what I'd said.

"I guess I do need to forgive her," she agreed. "I'll go ahead with her birthday party and find some other way to deal with the math problem."

While having a child make a C in math seems trivial to some, many parents withhold much more than a birthday party from a youngster who brings home less than straight A's. Why is that? The parents know their child has the potential to do better, that's true. But more than likely, the real problem lies with parental pride that's offended when children do less than their best. We need to examine *our* motives when we put such high demands on our children.

You Can't Retrieve Angry Words
Have you noticed how words spoken in hurt or anger are irre-

trievable? There's no cancelling them, no pretending we didn't say them. It's like cutting open a feather pillow and shaking it out. The feathers scatter to the four winds, and it's impossible to gather them up again.

When eighteen-year-old Ann came home from college for the Thanksgiving holidays, she dropped a bombshell on her parents. "Adam and I want to get married now that he's making $5 an hour," she announced.

Aghast, her mother, Denise, shot back an angry response. "When Adam's making $10 hour and knows what he wants to do with his life, come back and talk to me about marriage."

Denise wished she hadn't overreacted, that she could take back her angry words. Before leaving for college, her daughter had been a committed Christian, even spending a summer in Mexico as a missionary. Now she stopped going to church and was surrounded by negative influences. Denise wondered how she could repair the damage done by her hasty words.

"Have you and your husband talked to Ann's boyfriend or to the two of them together?" I asked her. "Have you explained the consequences of marriage when they're both so uncertain about what they want to do in life?"

"No, we haven't," Denise answered, "but should we interfere at this stage? What if Ann elopes and holds it against us for opposing their marriage? I'm not sure what to do."

"What have you got to lose by talking to her?" I asked. "It is biblical for Ann to want your blessing; she may even honor you by asking your advice. Your reasons for opposing the marriage are valid. You brought her up in the ways of the Lord, and she shouldn't marry an unbeliever. If you can respond with tough love and help her set some goals for her life, she might get a better picture of why she should wait."

Citing the principle of the power of agreement in Matthew 18:19 ["If two of you on earth agree about anything you ask for, it will be done for you by my Father in heaven"], I suggested she and her husband agree in prayer for their daughter. "Ask God to remind Ann of the call on her life, then trust Him to do it," I urged her.

Her parents talked with Ann, and they also prayed. A year later, the romance ended. Ann transferred to another college far away from Adam, and the relationship with her parents was restored.

Unconditional Love

Parents want the best for their children, and it is not surprising that their expectations are high. Neither is it surprising that those expectations occasionally get smashed. How do they react when their high hopes turn to disappointments? For Christians, there is one answer: the unconditional love of Christ.

When Jeanne moved with her husband to Japan, she prayed for healing of the rift with her teenage daughter Deb, who was staying behind to attend college. On more than one occasion during her stormy high school years, Deb had screamed, "I hate what you stand for, Mom! You're a hypocrite! How can you say you are a Christian when you yell at me so much?"

A few months into Deb's first year in college, she called her mother in Japan. "Mom, I'm expecting a baby," she reported.

Deb was dumbfounded when she heard her mother shriek with excitement, "Oh, I'm going to be a grandmother!" At that moment, it didn't occur to Jeanne to scold her daughter.

Her next words surprised Deb even more. "Darling, I can't wait to meet Jeff. I'll fly right home and give you the kind of wedding you've always dreamed of."

"You will?" Deb asked, incredulously. "Mom, you mean you aren't going to scream and yell at me? You will come meet Jeff and give me a wedding? Wow, I can't believe this is my mom!"

A few days later, Jeanne was in Oklahoma with Deb, helping with wedding plans. After spending a day with her future son-in-law, Jeanne assured Jeff of her feelings. "I couldn't have hand-picked a husband better suited for Deb. Welcome into our family!"

I asked Jeanne how she was able to respond so positively to Deb's situation of being pregnant out of wedlock. "After leaving the States, I did a lot of soul-searching about my poor witness to my daughter," she replied. "I realized that if she couldn't see Christ's love in my life, I had failed God. I asked Him to wash my heart clean, and I received His forgiveness."

"What about forgiving Deb?" I asked.

"I had forgiven Deb of all the things she'd done to exasperate me, and my heart was overflowing with love for her when she called," Jeanne explained. "Remember, I'd prayed a long time before that kind of response sprang forth spontaneously. All I could think about was, 'I'm going to be a grandmother!'—and I was excited about that prospect."

At last report, Jeanne and Deb had talked through their hurts, forgiven each other, and established a close mother-daughter relationship. Jeanne is delighted with her new grandbaby, and Deb and Jeff are now walking with the Lord.

Don't React—Respond

It's hard not to react negatively—speaking words we later wish we'd swallowed—when we see our children heading in a direction we know is wrong. Many parents today are faced with the decision of how to react to a variety of distressing situations:

- A child withdrawing from life because of rejection
- A single daughter using contraceptives
- A son living with his girlfriend (or vice-versa)
- A child making close friends among peers who are a negative influence
- A son or daughter following a homosexual lifestyle
- A child openly rebelling against Christian values taught at home
- A child in trouble with the law
- A child addicted to drugs or alcohol

When our children's lifestyles go against everything we believe or have taught them, keeping the lines of communication open is not easy. To remain loving without implying approval of their questionable behavior is as difficult as walking a tightrope.

The apostle Peter said, "If anyone speaks, he should do it as one speaking the very words of God" (1 Pet. 4:11). And the writer of Proverbs says of the virtuous woman, "She opens her mouth in wisdom, and the teaching of kindness is on her tongue" (Prov. 31:26, NASB). These scriptures encourage practical approaches when we are at a loss for the right words. Take time to pray and formulate a more loving response. Consider postponing the conversation rather than risk saying something destructive to the relationship.

One mother, faced with her daughter's elopement, told her, "Let's wait to discuss this until after I've absorbed the shock. This is hard for me; please give me some thinking time."

Another mom, shaken by a son's decision, said, "Son, this is important to me, but it's hard for me to talk about it right now. Can we discuss it in the morning?"

Failure Is Not Final

Many parents have prayed for years for their children, wanting them to be all God created them to be. Then sometimes they've watched helplessly when they floundered, threatening to throw away their lives in a moment of passion.

Mary Rae Deatrick, in her book, *Easing the Pain of Parenthood,* has a word for parents in panic situations:

> To tell your pregnant daughter, "I will not accept this," or to remark to your son on learning of his arrest, "I will not accept this," is foolishness indeed. We cannot stick our heads into our spiritual sandpile

and expect the circumstances to disappear while we are hiding.

However, we can add three words to the remark that will change the meaning entirely and bring hope and encouragement to both you and your child. Try saying, "I will not accept this *as the end.*"

Facing our emotions, facing facts, and accepting the circumstances opens the door to our casting the burden on the Lord in prayer. We are now ready to receive from God our comfort, our emotional healing and our guidance...Let us correct what we can correct, change what we can change, and forgive all the mess that is left over. I beseech you not to think of failure as final. If you have previously blown it with your child by speaking heart damaging words, express your grief to him (or her) and ask his forgiveness. Turn the tables on failure by walking in words of forgiveness and love. There are hundreds of words to choose from. Take your pick. For myself, I am particularly fond of *forgive* and *love* and *care* and *appreciate* and *respect* and *need*. They team especially well with *"I"* and *"you."* [2]

"We Told You So"

While driving me to a speaking engagement in Georgia recently, my friend Ginger told me she had been a disappointment to her parents. Their reaction had hurt her deeply. She frequently had gone against her parents' wishes. "Ginger, we told you so," they would say over and over when her willful ways led to trouble.

Ginger grew up, married, and moved away from her parents; but she couldn't escape her problems. "Early on, my marriage was in trouble; and my life was a mess," she told me. "I divorced Fred and moved to California with our eighteen-month-old daughter, Christin. My parents were against this, but I was determined to live life my own way."

On the West Coast, dating and partying with the "jet set" enticed Ginger; at last she could throw off the old restraints and live as she pleased. But it wasn't that simple. Christin, like any little child, had constant needs. Finding a suitable sitter for her became an on-going problem.

In the midst of her struggles, her father sent a letter that set off alarm bells in her heart. "Why don't you send Christin to Fred to raise?" he asked. "You're not in a place where you can be a good parent at this time. Please think seriously about it."

"I was furious at Dad's suggestion," Ginger said. "Yet I knew he was right. We finally reached a compromise agreement: I returned to Florida and accepted their offer to live in an apartment they owned and they kept Christin so I could finish college."

They Responded with Love

Ginger smiled as she remembered those days. "You know, God was at work in my life at that time, though I was unaware of it. My parents welcomed me back with open arms; not once did they say, 'Ginger, we told you so.' Their forgiveness and acceptance of me was the beginning of my getting my life together again."

She not only finished college successfully, but she began to see good qualities in Fred, who had become a Christian after their divorce. They remarried, and Ginger committed her life to Jesus, too.

"Both of my parents are dead now," Ginger said when we stopped for a coffee break. "But I'm grateful they forgave me and never dwelt on those miserable years of my rebellion. They began to respond to me with love instead of reacting in judgment."

"When God 'fills your well,' you have fresh water to give others," Ginger affirmed. "That's what He's done for me." Ginger now counsels women who are in the midst of marital and family problems, offering them hope and encouragement.

"I Will Never Reject You"

Somehow in our fallen humanity, we fear rejection like nothing else. When we feel rejected, it is as if our very life is being squeezed from us.

When Millie was a senior in high school she had an abortion. Three years later, she got pregnant again. This time she gave up her child for adoption. "You little tramp, how can you live like this, sleeping around with just anybody?" her mother Blanche yelled at her.

"I was so frustrated at times that I wanted her removed from my life," Blanche confessed to me. "I felt she would never change. But then God would speak to my heart about unconditional love, and I found myself once more releasing her to God. I'd ask Him to flood me with love and hope, and He always helped me."

One night when Millie was pregnant again, Blanche and her husband sat on the side of her bed talking with her. "Millie, honey, I forgive you," the father said.

"Millie, I will never reject you, no matter what," Blanche said, hugging her close. "Please forgive me for getting so angry with you."

"It's okay, Mom," she answered in a noncommital tone. Soon after that, Millie moved to the West Coast.

Later as the holidays approached, Blanche wrote her daughter: "Darling, for a Christmas gift this year, Dad and I want your forgiveness for all our shortcomings."

Two days later, the phone rang. Millie was crying on the other end. "Mom, Dad, I've already forgiven you," she said.

"It was a wonderful Christmas present," Blanche told me, showing me a picture of Millie. "Just as God gave us His Son on Christmas Day, I felt He'd given me back my daughter. She knows we don't approve of her lifestyle. But I know God is at work in her and in me, too."

The important thing is that Millie knows she is loved and accepted by her parents. Knowing that frees her to change.

Wrong Reaction—Permanent Harm

One winter evening after Paul Billheimer had published his now classic book, *Destined For the Throne,* he and his wife Jenny sat at our dining table discussing lessons they'd learned through many years of suffering. Paul, who had experienced heartache and betrayal by family members and friends, said something that so impressed me, I've never forgotten it.

"Only a wrong reaction can do us permanent harm," he said. *"By God's grace, we can control our reactions. We must learn to walk in forgiveness."*

Here was a man who walked in forgiveness with joy. Forgiveness and right responses go hand in hand.

Approach the Throne of Grace

Most parents remember negative things we've thought or said about our children. Why not ask God right now to make something beautiful from these ashes? We can relinquish all our hurt, pain, and disappointment to Jesus, our great high priest. Wallowing in our failures is a dead-end road. Instead, let the Lord minister fresh grace and encouragement to you through these comforting words:

> For we do not have a high priest who is unable to sympathize with our weaknesses, but we have one who has been tempted in every way, just as we are—yet was without sin. Let us then approach the throne of grace with confidence, so that we may receive mercy and find grace to help us in our time of need (Heb. 4:15,16).

Grace to help in our time of need. Grace—God's enablement to help us respond in love to our children. Grace—ask Him for it!

Prayer

Father, thank You for your unlimited grace. I now ask You to help me receive it, so that I can respond to my children with Jesus' love and acceptance. In His name, Amen.

Five

Forgiving Prodigal Children

"Son, you can't stay out all night, sleep half the day, and expect your brother to keep working for both of you." The father looked directly at his son. No anger, no meanness in his voice. Just firmness.

The boy backed away from his dad, underscoring his hostility by distancing himself physically from his father. "I hate this farm, and I'm sick of your nagging," he barked. "I'm getting out of here where I can be on my own. I don't have to take this stuff anymore. So give me what I'd get anyway when you die. The sooner the better."

The father reached for his shoulder, pain reflected in his eyes as his son sneered and again stepped back. "I hate to hear you say that, Son. It hurts me even more that you want to leave home. I don't know if I can quickly find a buyer for your part of the land and livestock. I love you, Son, and I wish you would reconsider your decision."

"My mind is made up," the boy snapped. "I've been thinking about this for a long time. I want my inheritance—and I want it now! I'm headed as far from home as I can get."

"Okay." The father quietly nodded his resignation. "I'll give you your inheritance," he said, his eyes never leaving his son's face.

Loving a Rebellious Child

This version of the Luke 15 account may not be exactly as Jesus related the story, but I believe it can help us identify how we'd feel in similar circumstances. Would you have given the family inheritance to your rebellious son, knowing he would probably squander it? Of course, this father already recognized his younger son's character weaknesses; he'd watched him at close range for years.

In Jesus' day, the father could give a child his inheritance anytime he requested it, but it was unheard of for a son—especially a younger one—to demand it. This showed great disrespect and dishonor. Sons were expected to remain and care for their aged parents, but obviously this one wasn't willing. His father could have written him off as a great embarrassment to the family or as a sluggard. [1]

While the younger son was *entitled* to his share of possessions, he had *no right to claim it* during his father's lifetime. "His conduct was heartless as regards his father and sinful as before God." [2] The father might determine how the inheritance eventually would be divided (the older son was entitled to a double portion), but he normally retained the income from it until his death. To give a younger son his portion of the inheritance just because he asked for it was highly unusual. Obviously, this son wanted to be free of restraints and spend the money as he pleased. [3]

The Father's Reaction

If you have a wayward child you need to forgive, I suggest you reread the parable of the prodigal son (Luke 15:11–31), taking note of how the *father* responded to his willful child. Some Bible scholars believe he had to divide his flocks and land and sell a portion to have the cash to give his headstrong son.

And did this son blow it! He spent his entire inheritance on reckless living in a distant land. What else would one expect from a rebellious, disrespectful son? When famine hit the land and he became destitute, he was willing to eat pods from the pigs' trough—a Jewish son couldn't sink much lower! However, no one gave him even one pod to eat.

Remembering that his father's hired servants were better off than he, he finally came to his senses and headed home. All the way, he rehearsed his speech, consigning himself to being a servant: "Father. . .I am no longer worthy to be called your son; make me like one of your hired men" (Luke 15:18,19).

The unbelievable happened. "While he was still a long way off, his father saw him and was filled with compassion for him; he ran to his son, threw his arms around him and kissed him" (v. 20).

I believe the father knew his son would eventually come home. I can envision him going out every morning, looking down the road, scanning the horizon, and saying to himself, "Is this the day? Is this the day my boy is coming home?"

Before the son came close to the house, the father spied him and was filled with compassion. Running to meet him, he threw his arms around him, kissing him over and over again.

Can't you picture the scene? Father and son walking home with their arms about each other. The son—dressed in rags, dirty, smelling like a pig pen. The stately father—wearing a fine robe, a signet ring on his finger, his hair and beard neatly groomed. What is more amazing, the father smothers the son with hugs and kisses—and he hasn't heard the boy's repentant speech yet!

Remorse overwhelmed the prodigal. Looking into his father's beaming face he confessed, "Father, I have sinned against heaven and against you. I am no longer worthy to be called your son"

(v. 21). But the father stopped him; he was not interested in the son's idea about becoming a servant. Nor did he suggest a probation period.

Relationship Restored

Calling his servants, the father issued his commands: "Quick! Bring the best robe and put it on him. Put a ring on his finger and sandals on his feet. Bring the fattened calf and kill it. Let's have a feast and celebrate. For this son of mine was dead and is alive again; he was lost and is found" (vv. 22–24).

Talk about restoration! The son received far more than he dreamed about while he was back in the pig pen:

- The best robe—a sign of distinction
- A signet ring—a sign of authority
- Sandals—appropriate for a son, not a barefoot servant
- A fattened calf—a special feast for an important person. [4]

Wait minute! What about all the money he threw away? What about the heartache and embarrassment he caused his father? I mean, suppose I had given my son $50,000 (there's no indication of how much money was involved); under similar conditions could I forgive such a debt? Could you?

Our attention, however, is not focused on the consequences of the son's actions; it is riveted on the father who felt *compassion* when he saw his son coming down the road. Before he knew whether or not the boy had a repentant heart, the father welcomed him home.

In this parable, Jesus illustrates how much our heavenly Father loves and forgives us. The analogy is clear: If we want to follow God's example of forgiveness, we must forgive and show compassion like the father did in this parable. We must receive forgiveness in the same way the son received it.

The Prodigals Are Coming

Prodigal children are coming home in droves these days. Some with regret and remorse, but not all with repentance. Some are still strung out on drugs. Some are pregnant but not married. Most are penniless. Others, with broken marriages, are returning and bringing their children with them because they have no other place to live.

No hard and fast principle applies to receiving home one's prodigal children. Every family must make that decision individually, seeking God's will through His Word and the Holy Spirit's direction through prayer.

Some families decide that the harmful influence on younger children at home is too great a risk to allow a prodigal to move back in. Other families receive a child who is addicted to drugs or alcohol in order to nurse him or her back to health.

Jane and her husband took back their son Jeff. They prayed over him and over the objects he had in his room. Jane fasted, interceded, and travailed in prayer on his behalf. With the authority of the name of Jesus, she fought the evil forces of darkness that had hooked her son on drugs. Even when he was stoned, roaring off on his motorcycle, she continually prayed two prayers:

1. *"God, I free you to do anything you have to do to make Jeff a man of God.* **(A prayer of relinquishment.)**

2. *"God, come and establish your throne in Jeff's life."* **(A prayer of faith,** based on God's promise's that it is not His will that anyone perish [2 Pet. 3:9] and that Jesus Christ as Lord wants to rule and reign in every individual's life.)

Many months later, when he overdosed on drugs, Jeff sought help. A nearby Christian befriended him, pointed him toward Jesus, and was instrumental in Jane's prayers being answered. Now married with four children, Jeff continues to deepen his walk with the Lord, and the relationship with his parents has been healed.

A Lost Son

No pastor, counselor, or psychologist has yet been able to adequately explain why some children reared by loving parents with godly values go astray, while others from a more negative background do not. The fact is, some children from "good homes" abandon godly values, disappoint their parents, and wander in confusion before becoming willing to allow God to guide their lives. My friend Audrey has a son who went through this painful process.

A few days before eighteen-year-old Victor was to graduate from high school, he learned he'd failed his Advanced English course and would not be allowed to walk down the aisle with his classmates for commencement. Three days later Audrey found a note on the windshield of her small yellow station wagon.

"Mother, Dad . . . I have to get away. Don't worry, Vic," it read.

Audrey was shocked. "Vic had never given me any problem," she told me. "I had such high expectations that he would serve the Lord with all his heart in whatever career he chose. I had another child who was retarded, a husband who was terribly mixed up and not serving God, and now I had a lost son. I had to call on the Lord for help."

Audrey searched frantically for Victor, and finally located one of his close friends. "If you hear from Vic, please have him call home," she begged.

That night the phone rang. A weak voice on the other end of the line breathed a terse message: "Mom, I'm all right!" Vic cut the connection, leaving her no clue as to his whereabouts.

Immediate Forgiveness

"I had one choice, and I knew it," Audrey shared as she recalled the experience. "If I were to survive emotionally, I had to forgive Vic for the disappointment I felt because he was not graduating and for his leaving home without so much as a good-bye.

"I also had to lay down my pride, my hurt, and finally my anger. I'd be tormented over what he had done to me and worrying about where he was if I didn't. So, I made the choice: I forgave Vic, releasing all my pent-up feelings as I committed him once again into God's care."

From then on Audrey prayed tenaciously every day, but with open hands: "Lord you know where Vic is; I don't. Watch over him. Please see that he has a place to stay, clean sheets, food to eat."

"It Changed My Outlook"

Whenever Audrey drove past young men hitchhiking, she prayed for each one because, as she told me, "I knew my boy was probably out there somewhere, too. My whole outlook on runaways who thumb rides with strangers changed. To this day, I pray for hitchhikers on the side of the road."

Three months after his disappearance, Audrey woke up feeling she should contact a friend of Vic's who worked at a downtown music store. Without having any outside evidence, she believed her son was back in the area. That day, she found her son's friend in the music store and pushed a note into his hand. Her only words: "If you see Vic, please give him this."

The note read: "Vic, I'll come get you on Sunday for lunch. Mom." That evening, the friend called to say Vic would be ready at noon on Sunday. He gave directions to his apartment in a bad section of town.

The following Sunday, Audrey asked her adult Sunday school class to pray for her. "I don't want to cry and fall apart when I see him," she told them.

When she drove up in front of the apartment, a frail, thin boy wearing a threadbare sweater climbed silently into her car. It had been ninety-four days since she had seen her son. "Hello, Vic."

"Hello, Mom. I missed you."

Those words from Vic opened the door for their relationship to begin mending. Audrey received him with love and resisted plying him with questions about why he ran away.

At home, Vic devoured her fried chicken, rice, gravy, corn-bread, and black-eyed peas. For a few minutes, only his teary eyes could express his gratitude. Finally able to speak, he said, "Mom, this is so good. I want you to know there was never a night when I didn't have a place to stay with clean sheets. I always had food of some kind."

What a God! Awareness of the Father's goodness swept over Audrey, igniting her heart with praise for answered prayer. As they talked, she learned Vic had left North Carolina with only twenty-three dollars in his pocket, hitchhiked first to New York and then to New Mexico. Overwhelmed with failure when he couldn't graduate, he chose to run rather than face anybody. Now he was back in town, holding down a menial job.

A Long Road to Restoration

After Vic left, Audrey turned to her husband. "Aren't you going to invite him to move back home?"

"Absolutely not." No room for negotiation in his answer. "The boy left on his own. He chose to run away—let him make it on his own."

The next Sunday, Audrey again invited Vic for lunch. Again when she asked her husband to let him move back, he shouted, "No. No. No!"

Six weeks later, after much prayer on Audrey's part, her husband asked Vic to move back home; and he did. Audrey drove him to night school until he earned his high school diploma. He enrolled in a junior college and later in a technical college. A short, unhappy marriage ended in divorce, but his mother never stopped praying for her willful son.

At age twenty-eight, Vic committed his life to the Lord Jesus. A few years later, he married a wonderful Christian girl from Belgium. Throughout their beautiful wedding ceremony, all Audrey could do was whisper, "Thank you. Thank you. Thank you, Lord."

As we talked about Vic's transformation, Audrey was emphatic about the relationship of love and forgiveness. "If you are going to *love* your children, no matter what they do, you have to *forgive* them," she said. "I'd be fooling myself if I didn't admit there were plenty of times I had to forgive Vic, even after he moved back home. His first broken marriage was heartbreaking to me, and it seemed he was in the enemy's territory for a long, long time. I had to keep on forgiving him—but I'm glad I did. Thank God for His faithfulness."

This prodigal son not only returned to the bosom of his family, but came all the way home to his heavenly Father.

Hoping for Good News

Rhonda, a sixteen-year-old junior in high school, was the only one of Nancy's three that was a "problem child." Although she never got in trouble with the law, she continually rebelled against her parent's rules, argued, and generally kept things in an uproar when she was home.

One Friday night, she didn't come home following a football game. Long past her curfew, Nancy called the home of the girlfriend who had picked Rhonda up that evening. Neither of the girls was there.

Saturday morning, the sleepless parents called the police to report the girls missing and the car stolen. For three days and nights, Nancy and her husband Rick barely slept. Rick drove around searching during the day, while Nancy stayed close to the phone, hoping for news... hoping, praying, and drinking dozens of cups of coffee.

On the fourth day, Rhonda called. "Mom, I'm coming home, okay?" she asked.

"Yes, yes, come home," Nancy cried. "Where are you?"

"In Pensacola."

"Are you all right?"

"Oh yeah, we're fine. We've been sleeping in the car."

"Please be careful—I'll be waiting for you," Nancy said.

Several hours later, Rhonda came in the front door. Nancy gasped when she saw her: matted hair, wrinkled clothes, and bleary eyes. "Honey, we were so worried about you," it was all she could manage to say as she grabbed her daughter and hugged her.

Nancy fought back anger boiling up within her. "I should be glad she's home, but she doesn't act as if she's done anything wrong," she fumed silently.

That evening, they read that a man suspected of murdering several Florida college girls had been arrested just two blocks from where Rhonda and her girlfriend had been sleeping in the car the previous night. Nancy's anger was tempered by that bit of news.

She rejoiced for God's protection over her daughter.

"Lord, How Can I Love Her?"

Nancy still needed to forgive Rhonda. In church the following Sunday, Nancy talked to God about her feelings.

"I don't even like Rhonda," she admitted to the Lord. "She's not pleasant to be around. The house is always in turmoil when she's home. Frankly, I don't think she even cares that she put us through so much anxiety by running away. Lord, how can I love her, let alone forgive her?"

The Holy Spirit's response was almost immediate. In her honest desperation, Nancy opened her heart to God and He turned back the clock in her mind to see Rhonda—apron wrapped about her waist—standing on a chair to dry dishes. Then she saw a flash of her bundled up with coat and mittens on a winter day, standing in the snow beside the laundry basket, handing Mom her brother's diapers to hang. She had been so lovable then! She saw her in the second grade bringing home a valentine with her picture on it that showed her grin with a missing front tooth. As the memories paraded through her mind, her heart softened. She remembered how much she'd loved Rhonda.

"Lord, restore that love to me," she prayed. "In the restoring of that love, I know forgiveness will come."

As she prayed, God sovereignly flooded Nancy's heart with love for Rhonda. Instant love—almost more than she could contain.

"Not only did I love her, I even liked her again. I forgave her, and I asked God to forgive me, too," Nancy told me.

Rhonda was one prodigal who returned without any significant sign of repentance, although she seemed glad to be back in the shelter of a loving home. But she continued doing daredevil things, keeping her parents anxious through her senior year. She went away to college, where she changed majors three times. Eventually, she graduated and moved to another city, where she has a well paying job.

"I look back to that Sunday in church when I asked God to renew my love for her. From that day, I was able to respond to her with genuine love and forgiveness," Nancy said. "Somewhere along the way, that love melted her heart. Now when she comes to visit us, she is a loving, caring, appreciative daughter. During one visit she said, 'Mom, I really put you through a lot in my teenage years, didn't I? I never said I was sorry. Please forgive me.' The forgiveness went full circle!"

What If He Doesn't Change?

Whether they change their ways or not, we must forgive our prodigal children. While the Bible does not specifically say David forgave his renegade son, some of the saddest words in the Bible are, "Oh, my son Absalom! My son, my son Absalom! If only I had died instead of you" (2 Sam. 18:33).

Absalom, the one who tried to wrest the throne from David, who killed one of his brothers, who slept on the rooftop with David's concubines as a public show of scorn—for this son David mourned. This prodigal did not changed his ways, but I believe David forgave him.

You may be waiting for a prodigal child to come home. You may look out your front window everyday asking yourself, "Is this the day? Is this the day my son, my daughter, is coming back from the land of the enemy?"

As a parent who stood in the gap and prayed for three prodigal children to come back to the Father's house and believed God's promise for the salvation of my family, let me encourage you. Keep praying. Keep battling the forces of darkness. Keep forgiving your children. Believe that God is big enough to use people and circumstances to turn their hearts toward Him—and home.

God can restore a wayward child to relationship with his family, if we're willing to love and forgive. Remember that our forgiveness will never equal that which God offers us and all our children.

Prayer

Lord Jesus, open our hearts as well as our homes to the children who leave home. Give us Your wisdom and discernment to help and guide them. May we have Your love for our children, even the rebellious, wayward ones. We believe Your word and that nothing is impossible with You. We expect You to enable us to communicate with those in our family who need Your love. We anticipate the day when, through prayer and faith, our prodigal children will turn their hearts toward You. Thank You, Lord. We praise You in advance for what You are doing in them to draw them to Jesus Christ. In His name, Amen.

<u>Six</u>

Favoritism

If you've stood at the edge of Arizona's Grand Canyon you know what a chasm looks like. One big, cavernous gap in the earth gives graphic evidence of nature's power at work. Not so visible, but just as real, are the "gaps" within our families—gaps in how we perceive and love each other.

As parents, we assume our perception of each child is the "real" one. Our children, for a variety of reasons, perceive themselves in a different way. When no one knows what's going on inside the other person, the "gaps" in our perception widen to misunderstanding and deep hurt.

Not long ago, my friend Dede shared how this gap appeared in her family.

"My younger brother got into trouble a lot, so my parents had to spend hours and hours with him," Dede explained. "I tried desperately to obey and please my parents so they wouldn't be disappointed in me. Years later at a family reunion, my brother said to me, 'Sis, you were always the family favorite. You were Miss Goody Two Shoes, and the folks loved you best.'

"I thought he was kidding. In my mind, *he* was the favorite. After all, my parents gave him all their attention; I believed they definitely preferred him over me.

"It had been almost twenty years since we'd left home, but neither of us had ever been open about our feelings. Last summer at the reunion, we both admitted feeling less loved or accepted than the other one. Fortunately we were able to laugh about our perceptions."

Seeking Attention

Dede's experience touches on a common reality in families. Children often misbehave to draw attention to themselves. It could be out of their need for recognition, or it could be the result of parents' favoring (or "disfavoring") one or more of their children. The "problem child," perceiving this as rejection, will strive even harder for his parents' attention.

Let's be honest, parents are human with likes and dislikes. They are not immune to showing their preferences for behavior, personality, or appearance of one child over another. Either consciously or unconsciously, they could choose a "favorite" or "unfavorite."

A neat, obedient daughter is easier to accept and love than a son who is messy, disobedient, and sassy. And a son who makes excellent grades and shows respect for his parents will be more readily favored than a daughter who runs with a bad crowd, breaks curfew, and takes drugs.

What help is there for parents? Do we grit our teeth and overlook our children's faults or bad behavior? Do we deny our inclination to prefer one over another? Do we condemn ourselves for our feelings?

The apostle Paul comes to our rescue with a practical word for us: "I will show you the most excellent way" (1 Cor. 12:31). That way, parents, is to love our children with God's love—to make an exchange: our limited human love for His inexhaustible divine love.

Trying harder, denying our feelings, or castigating ourselves as "bad parents" will not do the job. God's love is our only answer to favoritism. He's always ready to give it.

Consider how He loves:

1. God has no favorites. He accepts and loves us all alike (see Acts 10:34,35).
2. God loves us unconditionally. He distinquishes us from our behavior, appearance, or personality; He simply loves us (see Jeremiah 31:3 and Romans 5:8).
3. God shares His love with us. He promises to pour His love into our hearts (see Romans 5:5). As parents, we need His unconditional love to override our human inclination to show preference within our families.

Extra Help to One in Need

Most parents don't intentionally set out to pick an "unfavorite" child. Life in a fallen world, however, often hits us with unexpected pressures and demands. Parents may find it difficult to forgive a child during a particular season in his life when he is requiring more time, attention, or money than the other children. A physical illness, an emotional breakdown, a bout with drugs, an accident, or a financial setback may require parents not only to forgive, but to give extra devotion to the one with the crucial need. Giving help to one child with a special need without seeming to neglect another is hard. Lori and Bowman know of this first-hand.

"When our older daughter was seriously ill some years ago, the next oldest told her younger brother, 'Mama and Daddy are so busy helping Kathy now, you and I will have to take care of each other.' "

Lori and Bowman were not aware of this until several years later, when, at a family conference, they were explaining how love reaches out to the one in need and how we all have a need sooner or later.

"It has continued to work out this way over the years," she explained. "Even materially speaking. We have bought furniture for one, appliances for another, clothes for another—and it all evens out somehow. I think the lack of jealousy among our three grown children goes back to that time of extreme need when Kathy was ill and the others recognized she needed special attention.

"As adults, they frequently help each other. They are all different, yet they are mature people who have come to appreciate one another's uniqueness. They understand that Bowman and I love each of them as individuals. We don't have favorites."

The "Unfavorite"

Florence confessed to me she struggled to *like* her youngest child, five-year-old Candy, whom she called the most "unfavorite" of her three. This was the child she yelled at the most, blamed the sibling squabbles on, and thought was unattractive. She felt it impossible to love her unconditionally.

I inquired about the conditions of this daughter's birth, and I learned that when Florence was pregnant with Candy, her husband left her for a younger woman. As we talked, Florence realized she had unconsciously attributed her husband's leaving to the fact that she was pregnant—large and unattractive. They divorced, and he later committed suicide. She was still taking out her resentment and hurt on the child she was carrying at the time her husband left—blaming her for the broken marriage.

When Florence identified that her own feelings blocked a loving relationship with Candy, she was heartsick but determined.

She acknowledged the time when she had let these feelings against Candy creep in. She prayed with a repentant heart, "Lord, I forgive my daughter. I forgive my husband. Please forgive me."

Later she wrote and told me her whole attitude toward Candy had changed. The Lord had baptized her with His love, and her "unlovable," five-year-old daughter became "lovable" in her eyes for the first time. Forgiveness made the difference.

Recognize Uniqueness

All children have different needs and must be dealt with on an individual basis.

"Recognizing the uniqueness of our children, their creative bent, is a key to avoiding the competitiveness that can develop between brothers and sisters," says Helen Hosier in *You Never Stop Being A Parent*. "We can't always treat them alike— temperamental differences come into play, as well as physiological and emotional variations. No two personalities are going to be exactly alike. [1]

If we are guilty of showing favoritism or if we have a favorite child and it shows consistently, we need to take care of that. "We must help each child understand that we love each of them, albeit sometimes that love gets shown in different ways," Helen Hosier continues.

"Sometimes one child does get favored—his or her circumstances may warrant it, may, in fact, dictate it—at other times, another child receives favored attention." [2]

One mother exclaimed, "There's no such thing as being fair. Trying to make everything absolutely equal among your children is impossible!"

That is true to a large degree. The question is, how do your children see you as a parent?

I once asked my son this question. During his adolescence he thought we were too strict with Quinett, his older sister, too lenient on the younger, Sherry. Since he was the middle child, he thought he was unfairly blamed for things. "Keith, all I can say is, 'I'm sorry; will you forgive me?' " I responded. And he did.

Quinett piped up, "Mom, I thought you treated us equally."
"Thanks," I sighed.

My friend Peggy has a unique relationship with each of her five children. "Each of my children thinks he or she is my favorite," she told me with a grin. "I think every child in the world wants to think he is his mother's most beloved. I've always worked hard at spending quality time with each one of mine, so each one thinks he or she is special. Also, I've tried to be genuinely interested in their activities, whether it was art, music, interior design, or tennis. Still I have to say, God is the one who gave me the creative ways to be the mother each of them needed."

Learning from Scripture

To help our children understand that we love each of them impartially is a challenge. In Scripture, we find an example from which we can learn.

"Isaac. . . loved Esau, but Rebekah loved Jacob" (Gen. 25:28). If Isaac and Rebekah each had a favorite son, they also each had an "unfavorite." Twin sons, each favored by one parent, created strife and jealousy that continued for years between their descendants.

The older of the two, Esau, was entitled to the birthright due the firstborn son, as well as the patriarchal blessing from Isaac. This meant he would inherit a double share of his father's property when Isaac died.

One day, however, he came in from hunting so desperately hungry that he sold his birthright to Jacob for a bowl of stew. Although he gave up his birthright, he still expected to receive his father's special blessing.

When Isaac felt he was about to die, he asked Esau to kill wild game and prepare him a tasty meal so that he might give Esau his blessing. Isaac's love for the wild meat his older son often prepared shows how selfish his favoritism for this child was: it was based on his own carnal appetite.

Rebekah, overhearing their conversation, sought to secure the blessing for her favorite, Jacob, the tent-dweller. She prepared the meal and instructed Jacob to disguise himself to resemble his hairy brother and to take the food in to Isaac, who was nearly blind.

Jacob was fearful that if the deceit were discovered, he might bring a curse upon his head, rather than a blessing.

"My son, let the curse fall on me," his mother replied. "Just do what I say" (Gen. 27:13).

Isaac discovered the deception, but only after he'd given Jacob the blessing due the firstborn. Once given, the blessing stood. Isaac declined to revoke it. Robbed of his blessing through his mother's cunning, Esau swore to kill his brother.

When she heard of Esau's plan, Rebekah urged Jacob to flee to her brother Laban, five hundred miles away. She figured he could stay there awhile, then return when Esau's anger cooled. "Why should I lose both of you in one day?" she reasoned (Gen. 27:45).

Second Blessing

Isaac summoned Jacob, commanded him not to marry a Canaanite woman while staying with his uncle, then sent him off with a powerful blessing.

What was meant as a brief visit turned out to last more than twenty years. The rest of the story is familiar. Jacob married his uncle's daughters, acquired a large family, and was returning to Canaan, when he learned Esau was approaching with four hundred men. In fear, he sent gifts to his brother hoping to appease his anger for the long-ago deception.

When they met, they wept on each other's shoulders. While it appeared that Esau forgave his brother, his offspring remained hostile toward Jacob's offspring for generations to follow, even to the time of Christ.

Did the Parents Forgive?

The Bible doesn't tell us whether Rebekah forgave her sons, but we do not see evidence of forgiveness—people released and set free. Had she forgiven Esau and Jacob, wouldn't she have attempted a reconciliation with her sons? We aren't told. Yet we do know she did *not* enjoy the fellowship of her children in later years; by the time Jacob returned home, she was in her grave.

Old Isaac, on the other hand, was still alive when Jacob came back to Canaan bringing his wives and many sons [the blessing had born much fruit]. Though the Bible doesn't say specifically that Isaac forgave Jacob, I strongly believe he did because (1) He pronounced a second blessing on Jacob even after he'd been deceived; and (2) He welcomed Jacob back home upon his return. Could a father who held unforgiveness against a son respond in such love?

Jacob Reaped What He Sowed

Many years later, Jacob was deceived by his own sons. The deceit stemmed from his favoring the youngest son, Joseph— the law of retribution in effect. In essence, he reaped what he had sown.

When Joseph's older brothers saw how their father favored the youngest above them, they plotted his death. Instead of killing him, they sold him into Egyptian slavery, took his treasured coat, smeared it with goat's blood, and took it home to Jacob to convince him Joseph had been killed by a wild animal (see Genesis 37).

Ultimately, the tragedy turned to blessing. Joseph reached a position where, in the midst of famine, he provided food from Egypt for his family back in Canaan. The family was reunited. But for years, Jacob suffered for his favoritism; he paid a high price for his unwise dealings with his sons.

However, he learned the importance of forgiveness. Before his death, he commissioned his sons to appeal for forgiveness from the one they had wronged. They took this message to Joseph from his father:

> "I ask you to forgive your brothers the sins and the wrongs they committed in treating you so badly. Now please forgive the sins of the servants of the God of your father" (Gen. 50:17).

Joseph set the example for forgiveness when he said to his brothers:

> "You intended to harm me, but God intended it for good. So then, don't be afraid. I will provide for you and your children" (Gen. 50:20,21).

Ask God for Creative Ideas

Isaac's, Rebekah's, and Jacob's partiality is a strong warning to all parents: we should have no favorites in the family. All should be loved equally and treated fairly. The good news is that God will forgive us for following self-centered, negative patterns, instead of being like Jesus who loves without favoritism.

Remember, our Father is not only forgiving, He is creative. If you are guilty of having shown favoritism in your family, ask Him for His creative help. You can rely on His wisdom and love to show you special ways to let each child know you are concerned about his or her interests, disappointments, and aspirations.

Sometimes you may need to say to your children, "Hey, I'm not perfect. I'm the first to admit it. But I love each of you in a special, unique way. I am asking God to help me to love you in a more supportive way."

Trust Him to do it.

Prayer

Father, may we, like You, be perpetual forgivers. Help us to show our children what precious gifts they are to us. Equip us to be better parents. If any of our children perceive themselves as unworthy or unloved, let us become aware so we can help reassure them of our love.

Thank You, Lord, for loving us unconditionally and for helping us to do the same for our children. We speak blessings upon all our children, and we thank You for sending them as blessings to us. Amen.

Seven

"Mom, Dad—I'm Pregnant"

"Mom, Dad...I'm pregnant!" That announcement thrills middle-aged parents like nothing else. Ordinarily calm, unemotional people have been known to cheer wildly, call their friends long distance, tell the checker at the supermarket—or anyone else who will listen: "We're expecting a grandchild!"

The prospect of seeing another generation ignites new hope, love, and purpose in parents' lives. *Your* daughter is going to have a baby and that news is just plain wonderful. Wonderful...unless. Unless your daughter is a teenager, an unmarried teenager.

Then those same words—"Mom, Dad...I'm pregnant"—strike at a deep-seated dread harbored in most parents' hearts. Shock waves roll over you. You feel like you've been kicked in the stomach. You want to scream, then cry as your feelings careen from denial to shame. From guilt to numbness. On to anger. As your emotional roller coaster jerks to a stop, a condemning question assaults your mind: "Where did we go wrong?"

We're living in times when thousands of parents have asked this question.

According to a twenty-year veteran with the Seattle Police Department, some disturbing things will happen in the United States in the next ten minutes: Twenty girls between ages fifteen and nineteen will give birth to illegitimate babies, while eight will have abortions. The U.S. abortion rate is estimated at four thousand a day; and, if the mother is a teen, she is four times more likely to attempt suicide. [1]

What Did We Do Wrong?

When Laurie, a thousand miles away in Bible school, called home weeping, her alarmed mother asked what was wrong. "Mom, I'm pregnant," Laurie blurted out. To which my friend Gay Lewis, mother of four daughters, responded with immediate anger.

"Not anger toward Laurie," she told me as we walked across the Florida conference grounds to attend a workshop. "Just anger. The kind that makes you want to throw the telephone through the window."

I buttoned my coat against the unexpected cold front blowing into eastern Florida and tried to imagine how Gay must have felt when her unexpected "storm" hit. Her own precious daughter was now a statistic, an unwed teen. Gay was powerless to do anything about it. Except be angry. Her anger was a mask for her wrenching pain.

We should not be surprised at the presence of anger in such situations, for as Christian psychologist Dr. Richard P. Walters says, "Anger and forgiving are intertwined. Anger leads to resentment, and resentment is rarely cleared up without forgiving." [2]

Parents who have dealt with pregnant-out-of-wedlock children tell me they first must deal with their own sense of failure, shame, and guilt, then with anger toward others for not understanding. They had to forgive their children, but that was only part of their battle. They also struggled with unforgiveness toward themselves and/or others who did not empathize with the crisis in their family.

Gay found this true in her case. Her life turned abruptly upside down. "What did we do wrong?" she and Tom asked themselves over and over. "Where did we fail? Why Laurie?"

For more than ten years, the Lewises had counseled and loved troubled young people; some had lived in their home as "extended family." They had seen every imaginable problem and watched the Lord turn the worst possible circumstances into examples of His love and forgiveness. Now the question haunted them: While spending time with the others, had they failed to give Laurie the attention she needed?

When Laurie asked her parents to forgive her for all the pain she caused, they responded more out of surprise than anything, "Of course, dear, you are forgiven." In writing to me about the experience, Gay said, "We lived with an attitude of forgiveness toward our children and all the wrong choices they would ever make. Forgiveness came automatically with each mistake. However, that attitude is not as magnanimous as it sounds. We were able to be forgiving because we'd already had to recognize and grapple with our own humanity and sinfulness. We had made plenty of mistakes of our own."

The Mourning Process

Overnight Laurie faced hard choices. When Laurie went for her pregnancy test and the social worker pressed her to consider abortion, she adamantly refused. Instead, she chose to stay in school where caring friends helped her through those early months.

Determined not to marry the baby's father, Laurie was left with a crucial decision: should she keep the baby or let it be adopted? The decision was Laurie's, but her parents assured her of their unwavering support, no matter what she decided.

"I feel as if I'm in a mourning process," Tom told Gay one evening. "I guess I'm mourning Laurie's losses more than anything. I'm sorry I wasn't more available to her last summer. I'm sorry her growing up came so soon and so abruptly."

He grinned. "There's one more loss—a really painful one—the death of our pride. But I'm not mourning that!"

Laurie stayed in Bible school as long as she could, came home to have the baby, and gave it up for adoption to a Christian couple. Today she is married to a dedicated Christian husband, and they have two children. In her book, *Bittersweet* (Bridge Publishers), Gay Lewis shares the family's experiences before and during Laurie's pregnancy and shows how God moved faithfully and mightily on their behalf.

According to Gay, the whole process of rearing children and moving in daily forgiveness begins with trust, learning the true meaning of that word as it applies to our children.

"Parents often put their offspring in bondage by telling them, 'I trust you.' The children understand that to mean, 'We taught you well; you know right from wrong. Now we expect you to always make the correct choices, the right decisions.'

"Then, when a child makes a wrong choice and fails her parents' trust, her guilt and shame keep her from the communication with them that could be so healing. Saying we 'trust them' doesn't mean we trust them to always make the right decisions. Our trust really rests in the Lord and in our children's hearts for Him. We have to trust Him to bring them to maturity, using their mistakes and ours along the way."

From a Father's Perspective

As we see from Tom Lewis' comments, a mother isn't the only one who suffers anguish when an unmarried daughter gets pregnant. Take Amy's dad, for instance. He wept bitterly every day for a week after Amy, a happy teenage college student, broke the news that she was pregnant. He found help at a Crisis

Pregnancy Center, where a counselor urged him to examine his own feelings. "I wanted to give my lovely daughter as a virgin to a Christian young man," he wrote. "Now I had lost that possibility. I wanted to experience the joy of my daughter's first child, but I couldn't do that either. I wanted to be a part of my first grandchild's life, but it appeared I had lost that opportunity, too. My tears weren't just for Amy, they were for me as well. I would also feel the shame and pain of her mistake." [3]

Amy's father had always had a subconscious fear that his children might engage in premarital sex. When his fear became a reality, "it was as though an instant in time stood still. I was numb," he said.

"I prayed for a spirit of forgiveness. Now more than ever, Amy needed my support, love, and acceptance. As I confessed my resentment and selfishness to God, He filled me with a supportive love for my daughter that I never thought possible. God's power of forgiveness took away the resentment. My emotional confusion began to fade. The act of forgiving put the choices that would have to be made into perspective." [4]

Forgiveness! God's agape love in action. Amy's father experienced what he thought impossible—a transformation of his own heart: the turning of his self-centered reaction to a supernatural supportive love for his daughter. Filled with the Lord's peace, he was able to express his new feelings to Amy in a letter. A portion of it reads:

"Remember, Amy, you have sought God's forgiveness and that means your slate is clean. So far as God is concerned, you've committed no sin, ever! Mom and I too, have forgiven you...What makes us proud, and God too, is the fact that you've acknowledged your error, sought God's forgiveness and committed your life to Him... If you decide on a placement plan, we will be there to support you, love you, weep with you and heal together." [5]

Tremendous words of encouragement from a forgiving, healing father! He later wrote, "We praise God for being the gracious forgiver and loving friend who lifts the fallen and restores a broken life." [6]

Forgiving a Daughter

In their book, *Why Wait?*, Josh McDowell and Dick Day point out that if ever there is a time when a girl needs the love, support and wise counsel of her parents, it is during an unplanned pregnancy. Because parents also are experiencing tremendous turmoil, they run the danger of reacting negatively rather than responding lovingly. McDowell lists some helpful principles for forgiving a daughter in this situation:

1. Take the initiative. Have you ever thought, 'Why should I forgive her? She hasn't even said she's sorry.' Remember, if God had waited for us to repent and ask His forgiveness before reaching out to us, we would still be lost. While we were yet sinners, Christ died for us.

2. Try to restore the relationship. Remember, the goal of forgiveness is reconciliation. So often when young people become involved sexually, the relationship with their parents is either strained or broken. If parents wait for their child to ask forgiveness first, reconciliation may never happen. *Forgiveness seeks reconciliation.*

3. Be genuinely forgiving. Forgiveness means to forgive from a debt... Forgiveness recognizes a wrong has been done but is willing to accept and forget. So many parents say they have forgiven, but they continue to hold the past over the heads of their children. Forgiveness means not keeping a scorecard... By giving our own acceptance and forgiveness, we provide them with a credible basis for understanding God's forgiveness. This truth is effective to the extent that we demonstrate it. [7]

Again we see the law of sowing and reaping. Forgiving and being forgiven. Setting free of a debt. Not keeping score. How right and freeing these principles are.

"I Laid Down My Pride"

When my friend Martha Jane learned her daughter Gail was pregnant, she felt her pride had been run over by a rock crusher. "No one can understand how the mother is hurt and humiliated," she told me.

"One moment you want to hold your daughter and weep, 'Poor baby!' The next moment, you cry, 'What will our relatives say? What will our friends say? How could she do this to me?'

"I finally laid down all my pride and became a loving buffer for my daughter—protecting her from the outside world. Gail enrolled in a school for unwed mothers and decided she would keep her baby. After her son was born, I took a leave of absence from teaching and stayed home with the baby so Gail could finish high school."

This proved to be the most effective time in Martha Jane's life. She propped up her Bible and read it aloud as she fed or rocked the baby. She memorized up to twenty-five chapters of Scripture—nourishing her own soul as she nourished her first grandchild with love. Hugging him close to her bosom and reading God's Word aloud, she began believing in her heart *who* she is in Jesus, that His promises in the Word are for her and her family.

The new grandbaby also affected her husband's life. He had been having affairs for years, now he stopped running around and their family drew closer together. Two years later, after the baby's father conquered his drug problem, Gail married him. They have a Christian home.

A Family Matter

Did the rest of the family have a hard time forgiving? How did they react?

Martha Jane's son was embarrassed when his sister became pregnant. At first, he went into a denial stage; but right after the baby was born, he went to see him in the hospital. One peek and he came away with acceptance. Martha Jane believes he forgave Gail at that time.

All members of a family facing a pregnancy out of wedlock must face the forgiveness issue, especially if theirs is a Christian household with other children.

One young teen said she felt her older sister disgraced everyone in the family by getting pregnant. "It went against everything we were taught, and I had to suffer for her wrongdoing by having people gossip about my sister and our family. Even though I was still a virgin, it seemed our whole family was shamed. It took me a while to forgive."

What About the Church Family?

As the Sunday morning service was beginning in my church recently, Merritt, a man well-known to all the church family, rose and asked permission to speak to the congregation. When the pastor called him forward, I noticed that everyone in Merritt's family was sitting together near the front; the three daughters weren't sitting in the youth section with their friends as they normally did. Something unusual was about to happen.

"Five months from now, our twenty-year-old daughter Terry will have a baby," Merritt announced in a quiet voice. A shocked silence fell over the congregation.

"She is moving home so her mom and I can take care of her. She is not marrying the boy. Young people, don't think it can't happen to you. Just one night's indiscretion can result in a pregnancy." The young people, many of whom had been in school with Terry, looked at one another in disbelief. Some of the girls started crying.

"We love our daughter, and we are standing with her," Merritt continued, struggling to hold back tears. "I don't want to hear any gossip about this. That's why we've laid our hearts before you. We've forgiven our daughter, and we ask you to forgive, too."

His wife stood and faced the congregation. "We have forgiven Terry," she said, "but I want to tell her again publicly." Looking directly at her daughter, with tears in her eyes, she said, "Terry, I forgive you, and God forgives you. The baby you are carrying is bone of my bone and flesh of my flesh. Satan doesn't give life; only God gives life. Your dad and I have agreed to help you raise your baby. We will always be here for you and your sisters, and we will stick together."

By the time she sat down, almost everyone in the room was crying. It was the first time I heard parents publicly forgive a child in these circumstances. Yet, aren't we, the congregation, their family, too? Of course we are. We should help bear the burden of praying for them in the difficult days ahead.

At the end of that service, many people stood in line to give Terry a hug and weep with her. The tiny redhead shook with sobs as I held her and whispered, "We love you, Terry. We will be here if you need us."

A few weeks later at a covered-dish luncheon, her mother told me, "Terry's receiving love, not condemnation, from our friends and church family. If there is one word I dreaded, it was *shame*. But gratefully, *shame* has not entered in here. Terry is walking in forgiveness—God's forgiveness and ours."

Life Is Precious

Another family I know wrestled with the issue of abortion. When Bernice and Tim learned their fifteen-year-old daughter Cheryl was expecting a baby, Tim sought counsel from a doctor and a Christian lawyer.

Both advised abortion. The reasons: Cheryl was so young and had a promising life ahead. To them, abortion would be the simplest solution. She could get on with her life.

Bernice shared the story with me when I visited in her home one evening. We sat before a blazing fire in the den and looked over the notes Bernice had written since the day three years earlier when Cheryl had told her, "Mom, I'm pregnant."

Until this happened, Bernice frankly didn't know where she stood on the abortion issue. She talked to a pastor who clearly explained his position. He read her these verses from the Bible:

> "For you created my inmost being; you knit me together in my mother's womb. I praise you because I am fearfully and wonderfully made; your works are wonderful, I know that full well" (Ps. 139:13,14).

"The pastor convinced me that life is precious and that God has a plan for each person," she told me. "I realized that God knew us intimately from conception, and that a baby is a *life* even then—not just a clump of cells or a blob of tissue."

Her pastor asked her to read a fact sheet published by those interested in saving unborn babies. With shaking hands she read aloud in the pastor's office:

"A baby's heart is beating twenty-five days after conception... brain waves can be recorded in forty-five days...at forty-nine days, the baby resembles a miniature doll...by the eighth week, it responds to touch and pain." [8]

While he didn't force Bernice to take a stand, the pastor's words hit her heart like a hammer: "God wants you to decide where you stand on abortion. When you have decided, ask yourself what you are going to do about your daughter's pregnancy."

Deciding About Abortion

Bernice went home and told her husband she would not participate in helping Cheryl get an abortion. She would help care for Cheryl afterward, but she would not accompany them to the clinic.

Tim insisted he wanted what was best for his daughter, but he pressed Cheryl to make a decision soon. Meanwhile, Bernice's close Christian friends were praying Cheryl would make the choice God wanted her to make.

On the day Tim, Bernice, and Cheryl went to a lawyer for a final consultation, Tim pushed Cheryl for her answer. Still undecided, she hesitated and her dad decided for her. "You are going to have an abortion," he announced. Then he drove her to a health clinic and made an appointment for the procedure to be done.

On the afternoon scheduled for the abortion, a friend of Bernice's and her three-year-old toddler dropped by their home for a visit; she asked to talk with Cheryl.

"I really believe abortion is wrong, Cheryl," she said. "If you decide not to have one, I know a Christian family who would love to adopt your baby. Please consider it."

Cheryl played with the friend's toddler for a while, then went to her bedroom for some time alone. When her dad came to get her for the clinic appointment, she hung her head and said, "Dad, I can't. I just can't have an abortion."

Tim was so shocked and angry, he packed his bags and moved out of the house for two weeks. Cheryl went to an out-of-state Christian home for unwed mothers and asked that her baby be given to a childless Christian couple.

Her parents had the joy of holding Cheryl's daughter following her birth and again six weeks later when they returned with Cheryl to sign the adoption release papers. Cheryl moved back home and finished high school; today she is in college and hopes someday to have a Christian husband and family.

A Need to Be Loved

Bernice noticed a great maturing in Cheryl through the process of carrying and delivering a baby. Soon after coming home, she said, "Mom, if I'd had the abortion, I'd probably be back with the old crowd again, drinking and looking for acceptance. But not after all I went through to have the baby."

I searched Bernice's face for a moment as I warmed my hands at her fire. "Did you have a problem forgiving your daughter for getting pregnant?"

"No, not really," she responded. "I didn't get angry with Cheryl for letting this happen. I could understand her need to be loved and accepted by her friends. I'd felt the same way at her age; in fact, Tim and I got married when our baby was on the way. Our son married when his girlfriend got pregnant. With Cheryl, marriage wasn't an option. She and Rob had only a casual relationship; they were too young; and we had never met him."

"How did you face your need to forgive him?" I asked.

God Has a Purpose for You

Bernice rummaged through her box of notes and pulled out two sheets from a yellow legal pad on which she'd scratched a letter.

"Here's a copy of the letter I wrote to Rob when things were fresh on my mind and so close to my heart," she said, putting the folded letter into my lap.

> Dear Rob,
>
> This is not a letter of anger, resentment or bitterness. I am writing out of love—love for two young people who have made a mistake. I do not judge or condemn you or Cheryl, rather I forgive you. I hope both of you will have it in your hearts to forgive each other.
>
> There's a great lesson to be learned through this. I pray that you and Cheryl have been jolted into reality and will take a long, hard look at your lives. Where are you headed? What is your purpose?
>
> Cheryl's at peace. She has asked Jesus to forgive her, and she has received His forgiveness... If you haven't done this, I hope you will right now and know you are forgiven. God desires more than anything to be in control of the choices you make from now on. Turn your

life over to Jesus and ask Him to be in control—to lead and guide you in the way you should go.

Rob, I will continue to pray for you.

> With love,
> Bernice

That letter to a teenager she had never met—the father of her grandchild whom she will never see again—speaks more about forgiveness than some of us can dare to imagine.

The High Price of Self-Gratification

I've talked to many Christian parents with unmarried, pregnant daughters. All of them said they had tried to teach their children the Christian view of sex—that God blesses sex in the covenant of marriage; that God's Word clearly says premarital sex is outside His plan and therefore wrong. We live in an age when young people are faced with heavy peer pressure and a fast-paced lifestyle begging for instant sexual gratification. They are surrounded by a media-directed culture that enticingly shouts: "Go ahead. Everyone's doing it." And many young people—whether Christians or not—yield to that temptation. God, however, calls sex outside marriage "sin." He will judge it, as many young people learn to their sorrow.

One young woman wept as she told me about changing her mind regarding an abortion after she went into the clinic. She had already paid for the procedure, and the medical staff would not release her until the abortion had been performed. Not only was she living with deep regret, she was still alienated from her mother.

"My mother barely speaks to me because of what I did, and my brother hasn't spoken to me since the day I had the abortion," she said, sobbing in my arms. "I long for my mother just to put her arms around me. She says she loves me, but she can never forgive me. I know God forgives me. Why can't my mother? I'm *so lonesome!*" I tried to comfort her, but how I wished I could talk to her mother about forgiveness!

A Painful Mother's Day

"I always pushed aside the idea that my daughter might get pregnant before she married," Grace shared with me. "It happened: she got pregnant, but she decided to get an abortion. I pleaded with her not to do it, but she insisted. To keep her from going to some back-alley shop, I went with her to a clinic open on Sundays. She had her abortion on Mother's Day."

For Grace, dealing with the trauma of her daughter's decision to have an abortion was more difficult than learning she was pregnant. "But as a Christian mother, I could not withhold love and forgiveness," she told me. "I forgave my daughter, even though I was violently opposed to her decision. I asked God to forgive her for having an abortion, then I asked for forgiveness for my part in it.

"My daughter is thirty now, married but childless. Every year on Mother's Day, she gets sick over the memory of her sin. I've told her that her sin is covered by the blood of Jesus because she confessed and asked for forgiveness. Now she needs to forgive herself and receive God's healing."

Here is an example to all of us who may have harshly judged a daughter, a relative, or a friend's daughter for having an abortion. We must remember their pain is excruciating when they realize the significance of their decision. God help us not to increase that pain by rejecting them.

Scripture teaches that when an individual sins, those "who are spiritual should restore him gently. But watch yourself, or you also may be tempted. Carry each other's burdens, and in this way you will fulfill the law of Christ" (Gal. 6:1,2). For parents of unwed mothers, forgiveness, love, and support fulfill Christ's law.

Believe God To Restore

What about those who become pregnant out of wedlock and show no regret, remorse, or repentance? Do parents still have the obligation to forgive? Yes! God wants us to forgive our children in the same way He forgave us. And His way is to say, "Neither do I condemn you...Go now and leave your life of sin" (John 8:11).

Some years ago, a mother in my circle of friends discovered her unmarried son was about to be a father. She fasted, prayed, wept, and read her Bible for several days. Then God reminded her that years earlier He had promised that her son would be a committed and anointed man of God.

"I still stand on that promise in faith," she told our prayer group. "Someday my son will be an example of God's forgiving and restoring goodness. He hasn't repented yet nor asked for forgiveness. But he will, and God *will* restore."

Thank the Lord that He did not wait for us to repent and ask His forgiveness before sending His Son as an atoning sacrifice for our sins. Otherwise, we would still be lost. As parents, we have the responsibility—and the opportunity—to demonstrate this truth, God's way of forgiveness, to our children.

In God's economy, pain and problems need not be wasted. Our heartaches can be times of learning and training for future usefulness. That's what happened with Gay, Martha Jane, Bernice, Grace, and their daughters. As God brought healing and restoration in their families, they have become instruments to help others.

"Forgiving is something we do by choice; forgiveness is something we receive by grace," a wise man once said.

Prayer
Lord, by an act of my will, I choose to forgive my child for having sex outside of marriage. I acknowledge that it is a sin, grievous to you. I ask you to forgive her/him. I also forgive the young man/woman who was involved. I ask you to forgive him/her.

Lord, I ask your protection over my child and over my new grandchild. Heal broken relationships in our family. Help us not to become bitter when others don't understand what we are going through. Lord, help me to walk in forgiveness.

Thank you for forgiving me and our family for the times we have failed one another and for the times we have failed you, heavenly Father. Make something beautiful out of this ordeal we're walking through. Bring healing to all of us. I ask you to do this in the name of Jesus. Amen.

Eight

"Mom, Dad—I'm Gay"

If there is a greater parental fear than learning a daughter is pregnant out of wedlock, it has to be the dread of discovering a son or daughter is gay.

When his son married young because he'd gotten his girlfriend pregnant, one minister said, "Well, at least it's a relief to know he's not gay." His remark is typical of the psychological defense mechanism parents often use to protect themselves from emotional pain in such a circumstance. At the same time, it indicates the deep fear lurking in many Christian parents' minds that their son or daughter might choose a homosexual lifestyle.

Separate the Sin from the Son

One Christian father found his son was gay and immediately asked himself and God a thousand times, "Why this? Why John?"

"I realized I never thought about the sexual lives of my other older children. I saw them as my children and only incidentally as heterosexuals. But now I saw John as a homosexual whom I was stuck with as a son. I had let that little word *gay* turn everything upside down. I was looking at the sin instead of the son.

"When I separated the two, I could forgive John. For the first time in thirty-six hours, a feeling of fatherly love burst loose in my heart. Forgiveness had given me the feelings to back up the empty words—he was my son no matter what." [1]

Later that day, when the father shared his forgiveness with John, they began to rebuild a loving relationship. Not long after, John turned to God for forgiveness, too. He still has a homosexual orientation, but he is now a Christian and a nonpracticing homosexual. [2]

The Bible Calls It Wrong

Most Christian parents have a clear understanding of what the Bible has to say about homosexuality. They know Scripture speaks strongly against it. In fact, according to the Mosaic Law, homosexuality carried a stiff penalty—death!

"If a man lies with a man as one lies with a woman, both of them have done what is detestable. They must be put to death; their blood will be on their own heads" (Lev. 20:13).

Hurting parents of homosexuals don't need anyone to tell them that unchecked lusts lead to perversion. They know it. They also know the New Testament says that when a man or woman chooses to exchange natural relations for unnatural ones, he or she exchanges the truth of God for a lie and becomes deceived (Rom. 1:24–27). But knowing these things doesn't alleviate the helplessness and intense emotional pain they feel. Only the ministry of the Holy Spirit can do that.

Emotional Pain

One pastor's wife, open about the emotional pain she felt,

shared her experience of dealing with her son's homosexuality. Here is her story:

"When you finally learn the truth about your child—usually after a long period of suspecting it but not wanting to face it—you are emotionally shattered. The pain is beyond description. You have a great fear that other members of the family and colleagues in the ministry will learn the terrible truth.

"In my case, it was a long time before I realized that the pain my son was feeling was equal to or deeper than my own. Ed masked his pain with anger and resentment toward me and his father. He lashed out at us to release his own frustration and despair.

"Hurting people hurt one another. We tended to respond with anger toward him which made matters worse. Then we would be overindulgent because we felt enormous guilt and a sense of failure as parents. We prayed desperately. Ed went to a Christian counselor for a year, which provided an outside person he could talk to. But he dropped out of church and began going to gay bars and running around with undesirable people.

The Work Of The Enemy

"There were times when I struggled with intense anger toward Ed. I sometimes felt he was rebelling against everything we ever believed in, all the values we held, as the ultimate means of hurting us and destroying his dad's ministry. At those times, I was tempted to blame my husband for not being a more attentive father. However, the Lord showed me that my adversary is the enemy of God in Ed's life and in our family. Not my son or my husband. My attitude changed.

"Later, when we could talk with him without getting angry, I began to see how much he had suffered as a teenager and to empathize with the enormous pain of rejection he had felt. He dropped out of church partly because he knows what the Word says about homosexuality, but also because he felt he would never find acceptance there. The only place he could feel acceptance was in the gay community.

" 'I have to be who I am, and this is the way I am,' he says. 'I wish it were different; but I've felt this way for as long as I can remember; and I can't change. I've asked God to change me, but He hasn't. So I have to live my life and try to be a better person in the areas in which I can change. The unhappiest years of my life were when I tried to deny that I'm gay. Since I've accepted it, I've been happy. I have a relationship based on mutual respect, not just sex.'

"Obviously our son is deceived by the enemy; we must continue to bind the spirit of deception that is lying to him and ask the Holy Spirit to reveal truth to him. Almost seven years have passed since Ed first told us he is gay. It has been a long, painful battle to pray for him, to stand in the gap for him. I have learned to lean on God like never before. My confidence in His faithfulness is rock-solid, and I refuse to be moved by visible circumstances.

"While Ed knows that we do not condone his lifestyle, he knows too that we love him deeply and have forgiven him. He has also forgiven us for mistakes we've made in the past.

"To other parents suffering this trauma with their children, I would like to offer assurance that as they place their confidence in God, continue to pray, and seek His help to walk in forgiveness, they will find a light of hope at the end of a very dark tunnel."

Without question, we Christians can resist Satan's work. We can pray and show compassion and understanding toward the sinner without allowing our mercy to overshadow God's principles in any area—whether it is lying, stealing, gossiping, overindulgence, adultery, or homosexuality. One homosexual who accepted Jesus and was delivered from perversion told a Christian friend he needed someone who would not accept his lifestyle, who was brave enough to tell him so and tell him why.

What Went Wrong?

Michael R. Saia, in his *Counseling the Homosexual*, says, "The homosexual must be ready to admit that his sexual lifestyle is wrong and be willing to forsake it before he can receive God's forgiveness for his sin." [3]

In examining the question, "What went wrong?" Saia says, "Usually. . .the homosexual man has had some kind of relationship problem with his father. Sometimes the father was gone entirely. Sometimes he was present but was uncommunicative with the children. In some cases the father was so volatile that the sensitive male child withdrew to protect himself. But there was some kind of breakdown in the father-son relationship." [4]

Saia says the development of the homosexual condition in the female child largely parallels that in the male child. "The same-sex parent is crucial to the process, so the mother-daughter relationship is the most important in this case, and the process of rejection is essentially the same. There are, however, a few major differences. . .Many male homosexuals have good relationships with their mothers, whereas most female homosexuals complain of mistreatment by their fathers." [5]

He goes on to say that most homosexual men he interviewed had their first homosexual experience when they were seeking affection, companionship, communication, identity, or security.

"He Never Paid Attention to Our Son"

I was traveling in the Midwest, speaking to women's groups, and had just arrived at the home where I was to stay in one city. I had barely hung up my coat when my hostess, Anna, blurted out her story.

"My twenty-three-year-old son is a homosexual, and it's all my husband's fault," she said as we sat on the side of the bed in the guest bedroom.

"He never paid attention to our son, never gave him a bath as a baby, never took him fishing when he was a youngster, never played softball with him when he was a teenager," she lamented. "It was as if he rejected him from the time I brought him home from the hospital wrapped in his tiny blue blanket. I thought he'd be thrilled with a son; but no, he never acted like our son was even part of the family."

I talked and prayed with Anna for over an hour. More than counseling from me, she needed to release her frustration. Two years before, she had made Jesus the Lord of her life, but she was still struggling with unforgiveness toward her husband. As we talked, she began to see things more objectively. She made a decision to take responsibility for her feelings: She would forgive her husband, forgive herself, and forgive her son. Unforgiveness is a heavy load. After Anna prayed a forgiveness prayer, that load was lifted.

"Remember, you must continually walk in forgiveness, whether your son and husband change their ways or not," I cautioned her. "Forgiveness is necessary so that *you* can be free; then you must trust God to work in the lives of your son and husband."

Neither her husband nor her son has yet changed, but Anna is free, with no more bitterness to carry around. When her son calls home, she always tells him, "I love you, and God loves you." He believes he can remain a homosexual and also be "a good Christian." That hurts Anna, but her prayers will follow her son, and God's grace will continue to pursue him.

When It's Your Daughter

Cora and Dan have six children, all of whom they faithfully took to church from the time they were babies. At seventeen, their second child, Donna, made a public commitment to follow Jesus at a large crusade meeting. The next week, at an out-of-town high school convention, an older girl lured her into her first lesbian experience.

That was twenty years ago. In the meantime, Donna had boyfriends in high school and later became engaged. When her fiance called off the marriage, she was overwhelmed with rejection and began turning to women for companionship.

For years, Cora and Dan didn't even suspect Donna's well-kept secret. But two years ago, when Donna brought her "friend" to her parents' spacious ranch for the holidays, Cora sat in the living room with them one night and confronted them point-blank about their lifestyle.

Yes, they admitted, they were practicing lesbians. In confronting them, Cora opened the Bible and read them passages which clearly speak against such practices. The young women, who are active in a large city church that caters to homosexuals, began to distort and reinterpret the Scriptures to try to prove that homosexuality is not a sin.

Believing For Complete Deliverance

After that visit, Cora told Donna her friend is no longer welcome to visit. "You can come anytime. But we are not going to allow this in our home."

"But, Mama, I want to share my life with you," Donna begged.

Cora hugged her daughter tightly. "Honey, I want to share my life with you, too," she said before Donna got into her car to leave. "But your dad and I have based our family life on God's standards, and His standards do not include the type of lifestyle you practice."

"I believe the devil has crept in and bound Donna's will and completely deceived her," Cora told me later. "I'm able to forgive her, but I'm also battling and believing for her complete deliverance. She loves the Lord, and, in fact, helped bring several members of our family to Him. She's my child, and I love her regardless of her behavior. I tell her over and over again how much I love her."

Whenever Cora and her husband pass through the city where Donna lives, they call and meet her for lunch; but they no longer go to her apartment for overnight visits.

Six months ago, during a service in which Cora's pastor asked all parents hurting for their children to come to the altar for prayer, Cora ran to get there. While kneeling, she once again surrendered Donna to the Lord. A blanket of peace fell over her, and she came away knowing God's answer was on the way.

AIDS Threat

With the rise of the deadly AIDS virus in the gay community, parents are not only having to forgive their gay children, but also forgive the sexual partners who may have given them the disease. One Christian mother, Denise, whose son Dean is dying of AIDS, told me she has sincerely forgiven him. And in doing so, she's been surprised by her own sense of compassion and appreciation for his much older "lover."

"I've come to believe that homosexual sin is the most extreme form of a low self-esteem—even the absence of esteem for one's own gender," she said when I saw her at a recent women's conference. "God told me He is going to use me to help homosexuals. To be truthful, my first response was, 'Yuk!' My next response was, 'Lord, how?' "

"Did He give you any indication?" I asked.

"He said, 'Just lift Me up—that's all,' " she answered.

She went on to say, "My son probably sees this man he lives with as a father figure. Although I know the relationship is a sin, I still appreciate the fact that he's been caring for Dean. Both of them have AIDS, and they want to come live with us. My son claims that he has returned to Jesus, and he expects to go to heaven. However, he is hopeful that the experimental drugs he is taking will heal him."

I asked what she was going to do about taking them into her home.

"My husband and I are praying about it," Denise responded. "We have a cottage behind our house; they could live there in separate quarters, yet be close to us. As it is, he's in California, and we're in Georgia. We don't feel we can abandon him at a time like this."

Other Factors

While some psychologists say that parental failure is a primary influence in a child's becoming a homosexual, there can be other factors.

Mike Williams, once a homosexual, now an evangelist, suggests that when a child is sexually molested, it is possible that unclean spirits transfer from the molester to the child. Williams was sexually abused by a homosexual when he was five. That started a lifestyle of torment. By the time he was nine, he was molested daily by older men in his community. He was warned not to tell, so he didn't even confide in his parents.

By age thirteen, he was having sexual relations with boys his own age. "At that period, my biggest desire was to die. I realized it was wrong, but I couldn't find anyone to help me."

Williams became manic-depressive and developed suicidal tendencies and low self-esteem. His greatest desire in life was to be "normal"—have a wife and family. When he told his family members he was homosexual, they turned away. Rejection, pain, and loneliness haunted him. Six times, he was hospitalized with emotional problems.

One August day in 1974, he was contemplating suicide. He stopped to see a friend, who offered to take him to see a Christian businessman he felt could help him.

"This man asked me if I wanted to be free," Williams reported. "I said yes, and he told me Jesus was going to set me free. He thanked the Lord for me. No one had ever done that before! Then he prayed with me. He began to address the evil spirits in me, commanding them in the name of Jesus Christ to come out.

"Every time he addressed the spirits, I felt this thing lurching inside me. I could feel pressure building up in my body. Suddenly all the air heaved out of my lungs and I was submerged with peace. I was free! Jesus set me free."

The businessman then prayed for God to give Williams normal, natural desires for his wife, Hazel. Two months later, his miracle came; the couple was reunited. Today they have three children.

Williams says a large percentage of the gays he has talked with were sexually molested as children. "I believe it is an unclean spirit which is passed from one person to another. To be really free, you have to get free of that spirit. Jesus came to set the captives free. He is the answer—the only answer." [6]

A Double Life

Jerry Arterburn, reared in a Christian home in Texas, confirms the connection of childhood molestation with homosexuality. He was molested as a very young boy, however he kept it hidden. In his late twenties, he turned to a homosexual lifestyle. After a few years, he returned to fellowship with the Lord, but the magnetic attraction of the gay world continued to pull him back. He found himself living a double life. On one hand, he attended church and kept up a facade of being a Christian; on the other hand, he lived another life in the gay world.

In his book, *How Will I Tell My Mother?*, Jerry tells his story with brutal frankness:

"I knew from the very beginning that what I was doing was wrong. There was never any doubt in my mind that this was not the way God intended for His children to live. . . I knew deep down that it was sin. But I refused to act on that knowledge. The attraction of the homosexual world was more powerful than my desire to do what was right.

"Instead of resisting the gay world, I clung to it for a new sense of meaning in my life. . .That security, false and pretentious as it was, was hard to break away from or deny." [7]

Jerry finally left the homosexual world for a second time—this time determined to make it stick.

"My double life as a Christian and a practicing homosexual had become too much for me to bear," he wrote. "I could no longer tolerate believing one set of values and living another. I didn't feel hypocritical, I felt fraudulent... I had had enough of misery. My conscience screamed at me to change, and I had no choice but to listen." [8]

The Deadly Virus

Jerry found that Christ was the only way out; but by this time, he was infected with the AIDS virus. He did his best to live a Christian life and suffered in silence for over a year, not sharing his secret with his family or anyone else.

He ended up in the hospital, totally helpless, but not without hope; God had ministered an incredible, comforting peace to him. Though physically weak, he grew spiritually strong. Eventually the nurse called his parents and asked them to come. Jerry would have to tell them the terrible truth. Their response amazed him.

"They walked to my bed with their shining faces glowing. They couldn't have hidden their expressions of love even if they tried. We hugged each other, and all of us began to cry. Then I looked my mother in the eye and said what I believe she already had concluded. 'Mother, you have a very sick boy on your hands. I never wanted to have to tell you this, but I can't go another day without your knowing what I am experiencing. I am sorry to have to put you through this. I have the virus. I have AIDS.'

"From the first moment they heard the devastating news, they supported me. They hugged me and told me that nothing I had ever done or would do would prevent them from loving me. They said they wanted to help me. They said they would hang in there with me and back me all the way. They wanted us to be a team. Then they asked me to go home with them. Unless one has been in that situation, it's difficult to imagine what that meant to me.

"My parents weren't ashamed to take me back. I knew they loved me, but the intensity of their ability to care about me was overwhelming. Those two Christians, both incredible witnesses for God, set out to support their homosexual son in every way possible. It was incredible to experience that kind of love and acceptance. In spite of the hurt they felt, in spite of the ramifications that news of AIDS would engender in a small Texas town, they did what God did—they loved me anyway. They reacted in direct opposition to the way the world reacts." [9]

Because of loving, forgiving parents, this young man experienced emotional healing. Though the physical healing he desired did not happen, he never lost faith in God. Jerry died on June 12, 1988. Before his death he wrote:

"In a sense I am grateful for my disease. Before it, I never dealt with the reality of life. I skipped through life with an egotistical misunderstanding of what it was all about. The disease has forced me back to the essential truths of life, truths that I found in the teachings and the life of Christ. *I would truly rather live two or three more days with His Spirit in me than spend another thirty-six years the way I was living.* The old way just is not worth it." [10]

A Crushed and Broken Mother

In the foreword to his book, Jerry's mother, Clara Arterburn, writes of the anguish she went through concerning her middle son:

"The news that Jerry was homosexual came as a total shock. I was filled with fear and disbelief. I felt betrayed, trapped, and frightened. Many emotions were released in me—guilt, shame, anger, failure, self-pity, dread. I felt torn, fragmented, wounded, and mentally helpless. For someone without faith in a forgiving God, it might have been easier to die or lose her mind. But God is the Lord of my life and the Lord of my family, and I did not die or go insane. With His help, I am surviving. Not only was

I pained to discover that Jerry was homosexual, I was anguished to learn that he had the deadly virus AIDS.

"I know what it means to be a crushed and broken mother. I also know the grace of God in this situation. The AIDS virus has hurt Jerry both mentally and physically. I am grateful he is spiritually a whole person in Jesus Christ . . . Not only has Jerry made his life right with God, he has asked our forgiveness; and we have given it.

"God's loving mercy is the most outstanding gift I have ever known. I have learned that when God gives a mother a child, He gives love for that child regardless of the circumstances of that child's life. It is God alone who makes a mother." [11]

Forgive Your Child, the Partner, Your Spouse

If you have a homosexual child, it is important that you forgive your child, his/her sexual partner, yourself, and your spouse. Accept God's forgiveness, too! Offer to find counseling if the child is willing, and never cease praying for your child's freedom. Christian parents are called to continually forgive and keep on trusting in God whether the child changes his lifestyle or not.

Prayer

Father, reveal to him/her by Your Spirit that You are the source of all he/she needs to obtain inner peace. I pray that _____ will desire acceptance from You more than acceptance from the homosexual world. Thank You that there is hope. Thank You for the promise that "the posterity of the righteous will be delivered" (Prov. 11:21, NKJV).

I will not give in to the enemy's plan for my child, because You have a better plan. Thank You that Jesus came to set the captives free. I claim that freedom for _____, in Jesus' name, Amen.

Nine

Forgiving Stepchildren

A million new stepchildren are blended into families each year in our nation. Experts estimate there are already eleven to thirteen million stepchildren. By the end of the decade, one in every three children will be affected by the divorce and remarriage of at least one of their natural parents. [1]

It would be naive to assume these children can go from one family situation to another without carrying their "luggage"—pain and brokenness—with them. Compound that factor with the role changes for everyone involved. Children who were once "the kids" become stepchildren, "his or hers;" parents who were previously "mom and dad" are now stepparents, "yours or mine." The whole new package is fragile at best.

While I was autographing books at a women's conference in New Orleans one fall, an attractive woman pushed a note into my hand. It read, *"Last year in Milwaukee, you prayed for me. My stepdaughter has not changed a bit. But I love her as my own.*

This time last year, I didn't. Thank you for praying with me to forgive her. God did the rest."

Is there a need for forgiveness in blended families? Yes, indeed—a crying need.

Obeying God

Another mother, this time in Georgia, stopped me in her church foyer to talk about her struggle to love and forgive a stepson. She tells the story in her own words:

"I was forty when I married, and I had no children of my own. Not long after our wedding, Dick, my husband's seventeen-year-old son, came to live with us. Because his mother was marrying for the third time, she asked us to take him.

"We soon discovered that Dick was not only using drugs, he was selling drugs from our house. One weekend, I found five-dollar bills scattered across his dresser. Some boy had come to pick up bags of marijuana and left the money for it.

"His father confronted him that evening. 'Dick, I know about your drug habit. Though I am not going to turn you over to the law, I will not permit drugs. I love you, and God loves you. But no more drugs!'

"Dick left our home, was arrested, and served a three-month jail sentence. He came back and asked our forgiveness, saying he had accepted Jesus. We still sensed an undercurrent of rebellion. In front of other people, he'd say hateful, humiliating things to me.

"I prayed long and hard about our relationship. One day, while he was in school, I felt the nudge of the Holy Spirit. 'Wash Dick's feet.'

" 'God, are you serious?' I asked. 'Do you want me literally to wash this boy's feet?'

"All day, I fought the idea. At two o'clock, I gave in. 'All right, Lord, if this is what You require. I'll do it. What if Dick won't let me? He's got his pride, too.'

"When Dick came in from school, I had a towel and a small plastic pan of water waiting in the living room.

" 'Dick, I want to wash your feet,' I told him.

" 'You want to what?' he sputtered, flabbergasted.

" 'Wash your feet. I have the water here. God wants me to do it. May I?'

" 'I guess so. . . I don't understand, but okay.'

"Slipping off his shoes and socks, I placed his feet in the pan of cool water, gently washing them. Still kneeling, I said, 'Dick, I forgive you and I love you.' I dried his feet with a towel, then wrapped my arms around his shoulders in a bear hug. Our eyes locked for one long moment. He picked up his shoes and socks and walked down the hall to his bedroom as if nothing unusual had happened.

"He never mentioned our foot-washing afternoon. Nor did I. But because of it, something broke in us. We both knew a wall between us had tumbled down. He never sassed me again. How beautifully God honored my obedience that hot spring afternoon."

Tenderness, humility, obedience—God wrapped it all up in the single act of foot washing and used it to blast away at the pain separating stepmother and stepson. This woman learned a valuable lesson: God uses forgiveness as a key to establishing a meaningful relationship with a stepchild.

Stepparent Myths

In their excellent book for mending and blending stepfamilies, *Successful Stepparenting,* Dr. David and Bonnie Juroe, who have eight children between them, dispel some myths about stepfamily situations.

Myth One: You have to be perfect. Instead, realize your limitations. Realize you are an outsider. Don't have unrealistic expectations.

Myth Two: Children can adapt easily in stepfamilies. The problem of adaptability is great for those entering into the stepfamily because their personalities are already pretty well molded. The children have developed needs, wants, habits, and coping mechanisms that may resist change.

Myth Three: Stepchildren quickly get over loss. When parents remarry, most children are bound to feel some jealousy and be envious if the noncustodial parent has bettered his lot in life materially and emotionally. Sometimes the loss of a parent never heals completely; we must respect the child who experiences it.

Myth Four: A stepfamily can operate like a normal family. A stepparent has assumed the responsibility for helping to raise another individual's children. Most of us have been conditioned to want our own children—not someone else's. A blended family is incredibly more complex because of the stressed emotional relationships.

Myth Five: Stepmothers are wicked creatures. Stepmothers often become the pivotal issue or battleground in the stepfamily. The home always seems to revolve around the mother figure no matter who she may be. If things go wrong, the stepmother is seen as the culprit. She may be a better cook, housekeeper, and friend than the birth mother. However, the key issue is not her ability but what the children want. Most stepmothers, however, have courage or they would not have accepted their role in the first place. [2]

Other ideas that the Juroes think need to be discussed with children pertain to a father remarrying and keeping his children with him. The children may falsely believe:

1. the new wife broke up their parents' marriage;
2. the new woman is keeping the father from going back to their mother; or
3. the stepmother is either ignorant or just plain dumb because she doesn't do things the way their mom used to. [3]

Displaced Anger

Family counselors tell us that stepchildren bring into a marriage emotions such as anger, fear, rejection, guilt, or grief over the loss of their other parent. Reacting from any of these, they may choose the stepparent or stepbrothers or sisters as targets of their aggression. [4]

A teenager may shout, "I don't have to mind you—you aren't my dad!" It's good to find out why children display hostility, then work toward a solution. Failure to understand the stepchildren's responses and reactions creates a further dilemma.

In some cases, a child may be angry with his or her own parent, but exhibit that anger toward the stepparent. Leah, who married in her mid-twenties and had two stepdaughters whose mother died, experienced this first hand.

"The shock of their mother's death and their sudden move to a strange town made the girls emotionally dependent on their father. When he married me, they felt they had to compete with me for his affection," Leah recounted. "I think they were angry at him for getting married again, but they took it out on me. The birth of my own child only created more competition for them."

The fact that Leah herself had come from a home where affection and emotional reinforcement was rarely expressed compounded the problem.

"I was too inexperienced at the time to realize how desperately the girls needed acceptance and emotional support," she told me. "I realize now I made a lot of mistakes, and my husband did, too. But we did the best we knew at the time.

"Now the older daughter is married and is a stepparent herself, so her attitude toward me has mellowed a lot. During a recent visit I apologized to her for the hurts I'd caused her and asked her to forgive me, which she did.

"She told me that when her dad married me, she felt he was thinking only of himself and not considering the needs of herself and her sister. That visit gave me understanding and compassion for what she had been through, and I feel closer to her than ever before. I am praying that the Lord will bring the healing in her life that she needs."

One Son Causes Turmoil

When Evie married the second time, she, her two children, and Eugene, an Air Force pilot, all moved from Virginia to Florida. Eugene had custody of his two youngsters, so they had two girls and two boys, all pre-adolescent.

"I whisked my children more than a thousand miles from where they had lived all their lives, away from family and friends," Evie told me. "Not only did they have to overcome homesickness, they had to cope with two strange kids in our home vying for my attention. It's a good thing I learned that I must continually forgive all of them, because at times I felt like choking them!"

Her son Sammy seemed to rebel more than the others, skipping school and escaping out his bedroom window night after night. Spankings and restrictions did no good. Eugene installed bolts on the window so he couldn't climb out. One summer when the family had planned a trip to Disney World, Sammy disappeared. Eugene stayed home to try to locate him, while Evie took the other three on a disappointing vacation by herself.

"Our house was a virtual tornado whenever Sammy was around," she said. "I found marijuana stowed inside his stereo speaker and once discovered it growing in his closet."

Exasperated, Evie and Eugene sent Sammy to live with his biological father in California, where he still lives. "When you have children, you have problems, and you have to continually forgive," Evie related. "I can't say it is easy. My problems with Sammy increased enormously after my second marriage. He couldn't adjust to a blended family. I took the easier route by sending him to live with his dad. I'd forgive him over and over, but I admit it was easier to forgive him after he was out of our house, no longer around to rebel against my authority or against Eugene. We've had a struggle in our relationship; but, when Eugene and

I went to see him recently, I felt our visit was a healing time for all of us."

No Role Model

"Some women think motherhood is the greatest calling in the world, but I didn't feel that way," Evie remembers. "I'm a task-oriented person. I don't relate well to people emotionally, and I didn't relate well to my children either."

Evie blames herself and her own childhood experiences for some of the problems she's had with her children and stepchildren. "When I was growing up we had no warm interpersonal relationships in our family of three girls. My parents provided food, clothing, and shelter, but no emotional support. I had no role model for how to relate to my two children, let alone to my two stepchildren. I was home a lot with them while their father was in the military.

"However, one good thing came out of this pressure cooker of trying to blend families. I came to know the Lord Jesus on a one-to-one level. It was He who gave me the capacity to forgive and keep on forgiving."

When a Spouse Rejects Stepchildren

Dozens of mothers have told me that their new husbands don't accept the children they (the wives) bring into the marriage. This pits the mother and children against the new "head of the house," often causing disruption in family life and division between husband and wife. Of course, it can be the other way around, too, with the father bringing his children into a new marriage with equal problems.

"All our fights are about the children," a stepmother admitted. One husband gave his wife an ultimatum, "If you can't love my children as you would love your own, then I don't want us to have children." Fear gripped her.

"What assurance did I have that I could love his children as much as I'd some day love my own? His were adolescents, and I wasn't even enjoying them that much, let alone loving them," she told me. This couple opted not to have any children because of the husband's attitude.

Loving God's Way

Obviously there is no one answer covering all stepparent problems. Forgiveness is essential, but another much-needed ingredient is *love, agape* love, that "seeks the welfare of all." [5]

Agape love is God's love, available only from Him.

The Word promises, "God has poured out His love into our hearts by the Holy Spirit, whom He has given us" (Rom. 5:5). Outside this love from God, little hope exists for us as parents or stepparents.

Agape love means loving no matter what, loving without hope of love in return, loving despite bad behavior. Unconditional love doesn't cut the person off when love is not reciprocal.

My prayer partner, Fran, who was both a stepchild and a stepparent, has a medical and counseling background enabling her to counsel many troubled parents. One winter morning over a pancake breakfast in a restaurant, we talked about loving within the blended family.

"Parental love, in its purest form, should offer unconditional love to its children—love that has no 'ifs' or 'whens' attached," she said. "However, few parents have experienced unconditional love themselves, so they *don't know how to give it.* Or they fail to express love in a way their children can receive and understand it.

"If we can scarcely give this quality of love to our own children, how much greater the problem of giving it to a stepchild who is out of favor," Fran told me.

"What do you mean?" I asked, glancing out the window at a raging rainstorm threatening to turn to sleet.

"Many blended families are like that turbulence out there," she replied, putting down her fork to stare at the rain. "They start out stormy, and then the atmosphere turns to ice."

Negative Personality Traits

"What about your own experience?" I asked, refilling both our coffee cups from the carafe on the table.

"I saw my husband Mike's charming ways in his son Mark, and I loved it. But then Mark would behave in a way so foreign to Mike, I knew that trait came from his mother, who in my mind was 'my competition.' I didn't like it, and I would tend to reject Mark because of it.

"We can usually identify with our natural children, so we often overlook or excuse their behavior. But it is hard for stepparents to accept the different personality and behavior traits in their stepchildren. These traits are foreign to their own genes or life experiences."

According to Fran, stepparenting problems are born out of fear, personal insecurity, inadequate parenting models, or selfish desires that take precedence over concern for the children.

"Stepparents don't consider the drastic hardship for the children when they divorce and remarry," Fran said, finishing her coffee. "If they did, they would try to cushion the shock for them and put forth a greater effort to make them feel loved and accepted."

Give Up Expectations

Another stepmother told me she finally decided she would stop expecting her stepchildren to love her as much as they love their real mother. "I no longer have those unreasonable expectations of their love," she said, "and it has freed me to be myself."

Still another said, "I got tired of my husband's young son threatening to go back to live with his grandparents, where he had lived after his mother deserted him. The next time he said he was going back to them, I set him on the counter, looked him straight in the eyes and said, "Murray, you are my son. The only son I will ever have. You can go back and visit your grandparents, but you're never going to live with them again. You are my son, and I love you." After that Murray never asked to go live with his grandparents.

If you are holding onto the hope that your stepchild will love you as much as he or she loves the natural parent or even as much as you truly love him or her, you may need to surrender that expectation until the Lord performs a heart-change in the child.

Some Stepchildren Love Back

Recently I shared a room at a retreat with Sherry and her seventeen-year-old stepdaughter, Rebekah. Their relationship is encouraging evidence that the picture of blended families is not always bleak. Some stepchildren genuinely love their stepparents.

Every night, Rebekah planted a big kiss on Sherry's cheek. "Good night, Mom," she'd say before switching off the bedside lamp. They wore each other's clothes, helped each other with makeup, laughed a lot and prayed together. Rebekah always called Sherry "Mom," but referred to her birth mother by her given name. Two years earlier, Rebekah had chosen to live with her father and Sherry because she felt that she would be accepted and loved for who she is, not what she could do. Jesus is the center of this home, and that makes all the difference in the world.

Sherry and Mike, both coming from broken marriages, were determined that the Bible would be their guidebook and Jesus their head. As a blended family, they are more than surviving—they are thriving, even with Sherry home-schooling three of the children.

God's Grace Is Sufficient

Stepfamilies especially need to recognize their need to be empowered by the Holy Spirit and be open to receive God's grace. No family situation is outside His love. In fact, the Lord has told us plainly, "My grace is sufficent for you" (2 Cor. 12:9).

"Grace is God's ability to do what I don't have the ability to do," evangelist Mike Williams told our church congregation recently. How we need that grace, *His* grace, working in us to enable us to forgive.

Keep Slate Clear

Sometimes we face family situations which underscore the need to keep the slate clean—to be sure we have no unforgiveness in our hearts. This was graphically illustrated to me last summer. This is a story about my prayer partner, Fran, and her husband Mike, wheelchair-bound since contracting polio as a young medical doctor.

Last summer, when he faced emergency open-heart surgery far from home, Mike's two adult children joined Fran at his hospital bedside the night before surgery. As the time approached for Mike to be medicated, Fran felt the Holy Spirit's leading to do something rather unexpected—to ask Mike's forgiveness for all of them. She wanted to be sure none of them would have regrets later should the surgery prove unsuccessful.

"Mike, we don't know what tomorrow holds," she said. "You could go to be with Jesus, or you could come back with us. I want to do something on behalf of the children and me. We ask your forgiveness for our not being what we should have been for you. Often we've failed you; other times we've deeply disappointed you. Please forgive us for every time we have let you down. Will you?"

"Of course I forgive you," Mike answered. "Will you forgive me for the times when I wasn't a good husband and father?"

"Yes," three voices responded in unison. Then Mike prayed aloud for all of them. They forgave and hugged one another midst many tears. Mike is regaining strength in a long and difficult recovery period following that surgery.

This forgiveness session in Mike's hospital room drew an entire family closer together. Like many of us, they needed to openly ask one another for forgiveness. Their's is a challenging example of God's love keeping the slate clean.

They Don't Know What They Are Doing

I'm always touched when I read Jesus' petition from the cross for those who were crucifying Him, *"Father, forgive them, for they do not know what they are doing"* (Luke 23:34).

We have endless opportunities to cry out to God on behalf of our children or stepchildren, "Father, forgive them, for they don't know what they are doing." Most of us, if we are honest, need to add a prayer for ourselves, "Father, forgive me for my wrong attitude toward them. Give me Your love with which to love them."

A growing host of Christian stepparents are choosing to walk in forgiveness toward their mate's children as they daily depend on the Lord for the strength, wisdom, and love needed to successfully blend their families.

Prayer

Lord, by an act of my will, I choose to forgive all in our household who have hurt me. Show me creative ways to express Your love and mine to each child. Lord, You know I sometimes become angry with them. I need to understand life in this household from Your perspective.

Father, help all of us to maintain genuine love and harmony in this home. Show me when to speak and when to be quiet; when to be firm and when to be lenient. Help me to communicate with my children and stepchildren what I am feeling, and let me allow them the same privilege. Thank You for all their positive characteristics and all the potential that is in their lives.

Lord, bless the one who gave birth to these stepchildren. May Jesus be Lord of all our lives. In His blessed name I pray, Amen.

Ten

Forgiving Adopted Children

"I'm so grateful to my adopted parents. Without them, I'd probably have grown up in foster homes all over the state. Besides meeting my physical needs, they gave me their family name, nurtured me with love, and led me to a relationship with God."

Adoption at its best! This adopted son's testimony illustrates what it should be. When you adopt a child, you take a stranger into your family as your own son or daughter. The Greek word which is translated "adoption" in the New Testament means "placing as a son," inferring that the adopted child has he same rights and privileges as birth children in the family. [1]

The first instance of biblical adoption is recorded in Genesis 48:5, when Jacob took Joseph's sons, Ephraim and Manassah, as his own. You will remember others: Pharoah's daughter adopted Moses (Ex. 2:10). Mordecai adopted Esther, his niece, (Esther 2:7). Adoption was not widely practiced by the Jews, but by foreigners or Jews influenced by foreign customs.

Adoption, A New Testament Picture

In the New Testament, adoption is described in terms of a new spiritual relationship. The apostle Paul stated that our entrance into God's family is through adoption (see Galatians 3:26–4:7).

Paul wrote, "He [God] predestined us to be adopted as his sons through Jesus Christ, in accordance with his pleasure and will" (Eph. 1:5). In Romans 8:15, we read that we have received the right to call God *"Abba,* Father"—our daddy. He accepts us into His family like adoptive parents accept a child into their family; we sense His gracious love in a climate of intimate trust and love. Through adoption, God becomes our Father; Jesus, our elder brother.

My friends Beth and Floyd adopted their daughter Sue after she was grown, married, and the mother of several children. Unusual, perhaps, yet they felt God wanted them to do it officially and legally, not just figuratively.

The lawyer handling the case told them, "Though you can disinherit your natural children, you can never disinherit an adopted child. Be sure you won't change your minds about this later." Beth and Floyd assured him they wouldn't change their minds.

"Something broke in Sue when she got the adoption papers saying she belonged to a family," Beth related. "She cried as loving acceptance replaced the pain of rejection. As for our family, we saw again God's love for us, His children. He never disinherits us!"

Special Problems

Parenting, at best, is never an easy job. But as many adoptive parents have discovered, rearing an adopted child often has its own special problems and pitfalls. This is not surprising when you think of the variety of reasons children are available for adoption. The most common are: illegitimate births, death of one or more birth parents, abandonment, or abuse. However, if parents choose to walk in forgiveness, recognizing that God can and will redeem our mistakes, the most seemingly hopeless situations can be transformed into blessings.

Several parents have told me they felt more wounded by their adopted children than by their natural children—possibly because they felt a greater sense of failure as adoptive parents. Some say failure was due partly to the fact that they had so wanted the adopted children, they may have overprotected or underdisciplined or overcompensated in rearing them. That doesn't change or lessen the hurt.

Lifelong Intercessor

A mother in South Carolina, for example, told me her two adopted teenagers nearly broke her heart with their rebellious actions and their ugly, unkind words.

Although she tried to bring them up as Christians, they rebelled and rejected her values. One day in her prayer time, she complained loudly to God. "Lord, you know how much trouble I went to to get these children. Why are there so many problems with them?"

"If ever I had a clear word from the Lord, it came at that moment," she told me. "He said, *'Not for your pleasure, but for your prayers.'*

"I forgave my adopted son and daughter for their rebellion. I understood that I was chosen to stand as a *lifelong intercessor* for them. Sometimes I get tired because progress is slow. Yet I praise Him for the 'natural' good I see in them, and I know that, in His perfect timing, we will all be one in the Spirit."

Her discovery will encourage any parent. Whether the child who has hurt you is adopted or is your natural child, look on the situation as an opportunity to be a lifelong intercessor.

Only the Grace of God

Virginia, a pastor's wife and friend of mine, has also experienced what it means to be a lifelong intercessor. Her twenty-two-year-old adopted daughter Melody has three children out of wedlock. Recently Melody became a Christian; but before she surrendered her life to Jesus, her parents endured eight years of rebellion, running away, illegitimate babies, and a flaunting of all their values.

How did they live through it?

"Only by the grace of God poured out on us through prayer, and through friends who loved us both, and through the knowledge that God was always standing with us no matter what," Virginia wrote when she told me her story.

"Melody and the babies lived with us most of the time, so it was essential we learn to forgive each other. I had to forgive myself for mistakes I had made. Though I had always had Melody's best interest at heart, I tried to control her, fearing she would make serious wrong choices. My deepest fear was that if her birth mother had been promiscuous, she might be too.

"She reacted to my control by rebelling even more. When I saw 'overcontrol' as my sin, I asked God to forgive me. I began releasing her to Him, trusting Him to work in her life."

According to Virginia, the most valuable lesson she learned was that she is not responsible for her child's choices. No one can make another person live responsibly.

"Although Melody was the mother of young children, she was immature herself. She often neglected doctor's appointments, failed to pay her bills, and was careless with her things and ours. I had to find a way to cope when I became angry, so I listed the ways she offended me. Then I forgave each offense. Daily I had to choose to forgive her for the anger and rejection she vented toward me.

"Since we lived together, I couldn't run away from my problem. It is very difficult to live with an uncooperative, rebellious child who is determined to destroy herself. But I learned to release my anger, bitterness, and resentment to God. My wrong responses are what God holds me accountable for."

A Helpful Method

The writer to the Hebrews gives us wise instruction in relationships: "See to it that no one misses the grace of God and that no bitter root grows up to cause trouble and defile many" (Heb. 12:15).

"That verse taught me that I had to deal with the hurt, resentment, and bitterness, or it would eat me up," Virginia wrote.

Her method of dealing with these things may be helpful for you to follow. She wrote out her wrong responses—self-pity, rejection, anger, resentment. Then she would pray, "Lord, I give these to you. Forgive me. I will not justify my wrong responses. Please change my feelings and give me your peace.

"As I forgave my daughter, her boyfriend, and his family, I believe it released grace *into* my situation so God could work on all of us," Virginia recounted. "Through prayer and lifting to Him each hurt that came to my memory, I was freed to forgive more easily the next time, because the pain of the past was being healed."

Spiritual Warfare

Virginia and her husband learned another important lesson in this trial: the necessity of spiritual warfare. "My husband and I launched a barrage of spiritual warfare early in our struggle for our daughter's soul and life," she wrote. "We realized our battle was not with Melody—or even her friends—but with powers of this dark world and spiritual forces of evil in the heavenly realms (see Ephesians 6:12).

"I'm convinced things would have been much worse had we not confronted the real enemy and had other people praying with us at each crisis in Melody's life. We have learned much over the past eight years about spiritual warfare and the power of God on behalf of His saints. This has been one of the greatest blessings from our trials."

Today, Virginia and her adopted daughter are friends—two adult women cooperating in rearing Melody's children while she continues her education, hoping to support her family someday.

Godly parenting is not for the fainthearted. Virginia's experience is a testimony to that fact. God never promised it would be easy, but take heart from this:

> "He himself has said, 'I will never leave you nor forsake you.' So we may boldly say, 'The Lord is my helper; I will not fear. What can man do to me?' "
> (Heb. 13:5,6, NKJV).

Charge It to Jesus

Sylvia, another mother of an adopted child, told me about her struggle to forgive her son Matthew. One summer evening she stood at her kitchen door watching Matthew, now thirty years old and married, jump into his compact car and speed angrily down her driveway.

"Why is there always a scene whenever he comes?" she asked herself wearily. Tears flowed down her face as she leaned against the doorway. "Why does he call me names and act so ungrateful about the things I've done for him? I can't seem to satisfy him."

Grabbing her Bible, Sylvia went out to the patio and her favorite lounge chair, the place she often went to pray.

"Lord, help me!" she cried. "I hurt so badly when Matthew says such ugly things to me. I'm having a hard time forgiving him for all the wounding words."

She began reading the short letter Paul wrote to him friend Philemon to ask him to take back his runaway slave Onesimus who had become a Christian. These words of the apostle Paul seemed to leap off the page straight into her heart:

> "If he has done you any wrong or owes you anything,
> charge it it to me...I will pay it back—not to men-
> tion that you owe me your very self" (Philem. 18,19).

It was as if Jesus Himself were saying to her, "If Matthew has done any wrong or owes you anything, charge it to Me, I will pay you back. But don't forget, you owe Me your very life."

Those words sparked a practical reaction in Sylvia. That afternoon, she had a long talk with the Lord, charging all Matthew's insults to Jesus' account. "I forgave Matthew and asked God to forgive him, too," she told me. "In doing so, I released Matthew for having consciously or unconsciously inflicted all those wounds on me through the years. Then I thanked God for allowing me to be his mother."

Sylvia learned a valuable lesson we can all benefit from: In our relationships, we must appropriate the reconciling power of the cross. God purposed that through Jesus all things should be completely reconciled to Himself (see Colossians 1:19,20).

We Did Our Best

One wounded, but healing, mother of an adopted daughter comments, "I came to the point where I realized God allowed us to adopt this girl. He knew exactly what family to put her into. We did our best in rearing her, and we are not failures as parents. We don't need to take on any guilt or shame because she chose to turn her back on us. I'm not sorry we adopted her, for even with the hurts, I still remember plenty of joys."

I don't want to leave the impression that adopted children cause parents more heartache than birth children. Many adoptive parents report that they have no more conflicts with adopted children than with their own.

My friend Fran recalls that some of her most memorable college weekends were those she spent with a classmate from nursing school.

"Though my girlfriend was adopted, she and her mother had a beautiful mother-daughter relationship. I saw firsthand what love and acceptace are all about. As a stepchild myself, from a completely different background, it gave me joy to be with that family."

Never Belonged

All of us want to feel "in," that we belong. Part of our natural drive is to feel secure and significant. We can emphathize with anyone who grew up feeling as if they were "on the outside."

"I never felt as if I belonged in my family," my friend Joyce told me. At fourteen, when she learned she was adopted, she was shocked. "I felt I *really* didn't belong because I was adopted. After I married and became a Christian, I went to my adoptive dad and told him I forgave his every offense—for he had been an abusive father. His response was, 'You were never anything but obedient and polite to me.' "

Joyce found her biological dad just before his death at age eighty-four. Unable to speak because of a debilitating stroke, he leaned against her shoulder and wept with joy when she asked, "Are you glad I came to see you?" Joyce told him she had long ago forgiven him for abandoning her. "I've prayed for you for years, Dad," she told him. "I'm glad we're finally together."

A stepsister she'd not met before, who watched their reunion, spoke up. "Dad had friends who kept track of you. He was so proud when you graduated from college and later married. He knew when you moved from our state. He knew every detail about you and shared with us in the event we should ever meet. He loved and cared for you, even though he never got to tell you so."

A Tender Father

The next day, as Joyce continued her vacation trip, she stopped to browse at an antique shop. Her eye was drawn to a nineteenth-century crosstitch that read, *"Love the Lord and He will be a*

132

tender Father to thee." Overwhelmed with a flood of emotion, she started to weep. God had been her tender Father all those years, lovingly watching over her when her natural father was absent.

Joyce adopted two children early in her marriage, so she has insights into adoption from both sides of the issue.

"When the adoptive child reaches adolescence and his or her individuality begins to blossom, the parent feels she doesn't know this human being," she told me. "The son or daughter seems like a stranger, with distinct personality traits unlike those of either adoptive parent. Fear strikes.

" 'Oh, she must be like her real mom or dad,' you say to yourself. It takes a lot of love, grace, and forgiveness to raise a child who has no genetic identification with you or your husband."

In some cases, the adoptive parents try too hard to be ideal parents. In their zeal, they end up smothering and then alienating their adoptive child. In other cases, when problems arise, the adoptive parents give up too easily with an attitude that says, "When they're not your own flesh and blood, it just isn't the same, so why try?"

Cross-Cultural Adoptions

Parents who adopt children from another culture face a particularly crucial challenge. They must try to make the child feel accepted, not only by their family, but also by the family's culture and society.

Some parents adopt a child from another culture out of a sense of nobility to help the orphaned and homeless, then discover they have problems they can't handle.

One white, upper middle-class family in California, with three children of their own, adopted a black Caribbean child. When he reached school age, they were shocked to have to deal with racial discrimination. They never anticipated the problem, and the mother found it impossible to deal with. The strain caused an already weak marriage to fail. The child felt the divorce was his fault and carried enormous guilt.

The father, a doctor, kept the adopted son. The boy is now gaining a sense of acceptance through his father's love and the help of a counselor. Willingness on the part of the adoptive mother to express forgiveness and unconditional love could have made an enormous difference for everyone involved.

Teaching Forgiveness

Patrick and Tommie, pastors in Arizona, adopted their Korean daughter Sally when she was four-and-a-half years old. The little girl had been found outside a police station in Seoul, Korea. When no one claimed her and a search turned up no relatives, she was sent to an orphanage "for the sake of her future," the record stated.

Adjustment in her new family wasn't easy for Sally. Patrick and Tommie encouraged her to share with them what she remembered of life in the Korean orphanage. It was soon apparent she had suffered many injustices.

"We began praying with her about these things," Tommie said, "and we explained that she needed to forgive those people who had hurt her. We led her in forgiveness prayers. She did forgive, and she continued to express forgiveness as she grew up and experienced hurt by childhood friends."

Were there the usual conflicts during adolescence?

"Well, Sally is a lot like me—a leader with her own ideas of how to do things," Tommie said. "Often her ideas were better than mine, but we would have conflict because of my wounded pride. I would always ask her to forgive me—just as I had done with all of our children."

Sally is now a well-adjusted young woman about to begin college. She has gone on mission outreaches with the church youth group and has been exposed to other cultures, a great help in giving her a broader worldview. Her spirit of compassion and insight into people's problems make her a gifted counselor for other young people. What is more, she is a delight to her parents.

In her younger days, Sally didn't want to acknowledge her Korean middle name; she wanted nothing to do with her Korean roots. Now she has a strong desire to return to Korea and take the gospel to her own people.

What a beautiful testimony to the power of forgiveness and unconditional love.

Surrender Heartaches to God

The Word of God tells us that we can cast all our anxiety on the Lord because He cares for us (1 Pet. 5:7). I believe that includes the hurts and heartaches our children have caused us. God not only heals broken hearts, He restores broken families. Stop right now and pray this prayer for your adopted child.

Prayer

Heavenly Father, thank You for the opportunity You gave me to rear this special child, _____. Lord, I thank You for the parents who brought him/her into the world, and I ask Your blessing on them. I thank You for all my child's good qualities: [name them to the Lord]. Please forgive me for holding grudges against _____ for the times he/she has disappointed me, disobeyed me, or deeply hurt me. [At this point, share with the Lord your innermost thoughts and frustrations about this child. He will understand.] Father, I choose to forgive _____, and I ask You to forgive him/her, too. I release my son/daughter to be all you created him/her to be, and I ask Your blessings to rest upon his/her life. In Jesus' name, Amen.

If You Gave Up a Child

Perhaps you are a parent who gave up a child for adoption. I urge you to pray for that child and to thank God for the home where he/she is now living. Pray for the adoptive parents. Pray for God's perfect will to be accomplished in your child's life. Thank Him for this child who is able to bless another family.

If you feel guilty, ask the Lord to remove guilt. You can claim 1 John 1:9: "If we confess our sins, he is faithful and just and will forgive us our sins and purify us from all unrighteousness." When He forgives you, there is no condemnation. You may need to forgive someone who was involved in the pregnancy or in the decision you made to release the child for adoption. Remember, the key to answered prayer is in harboring no unforgiveness!

Eleven

Forgiving Addicted Children

Any child in the United States between the ages of five and twenty-five will almost assuredly be exposed to drugs and will have to make an early decision whether or not to use them. Drug abuse is rampant—and spreading—in our nation's schools and work places.

Some young people see no reason why they should abstain from drugs—as this teen's letter to a syndicated columnist in our local newspaper indicates:

Dear Dr. Wallace:
"I am a drug user, and I enjoy my life very much. I smoke pot and snort cocaine regularly. I don't see what's wrong with my lifestyle. My parents smoke, drink, and consume coffee. My mom takes diet pills and sleeping pills, and my dad takes aspirin daily for his headaches. I take drugs—they take drugs—

what's the big deal? I'm a criminal, but they are model citizens. Todd, Calif. [1]

The drug epidemic has brought our nation to the verge of chaos. According to recent findings of Citizens for Drug Awareness, drug abuse is our number one problem. Consider these facts:

- Fifty percent of teen deaths are alcohol related.
- One out of every five high school students has a drinking problem.
- One-third of American children start smoking marijuana in grade school.
- More than seventy percent of high school seniors use drugs regularly.
- It takes an adult five to fifteen years from the time of his first drink to becoming an alcoholic, but it can take a teen only six to eighteen months and a pre-adolescent as little as three months from the time of a first drink to becoming a confirmed alcoholic. [2]

As concerned pastor Jamie Buckingham points out, the answer "is not to stop the flow of drugs into our nation, but to change hearts inside the nation. Jesus sent us to set the captives free, and no bondage is worse than addiction." [3]

Chemical abuse by one member of the family affects and wounds all other family members. The following story relates one family's heartache and how they learned to walk in forgiveness.

Don't Let It Be My Son

Leo and Sharon, exhausted from the busy day at their fast food restaurant, sprawled on their king-sized bed to watch the late news on television. The newscaster's tone was grim. "Local police are looking for two white males suspected of murdering a woman in front of her house when she surprised them this afternoon during a robbery," he reported. "The victim's name is being withheld.

Her young son, who witnessed the shooting, was unhurt. Officers have reason to believe the robbery was drug-related."

Leo shut off the television. In a surge of emotion, he pummeled his pillow with his clenched fist. "That better not be Nick. It better not be my son," he repeated to himself. "I couldn't stand it if our own flesh and blood murdered for drugs. Oh, God, forgive me for even thinking it could be Nick. Please be with Nick, Lord, wherever he is right now. Be with our other sons, too."

Leo punched his pillow again. He needed sleep, but his mind wouldn't stop; it kept racing over the past few years of Nick's life. At seventeen, he'd tricked his parents into letting him get married, saying his fifteen-year-old girlfriend was pregnant. She wasn't. Within the next five years, they had three children. Nick had brushes with the law, resulting in two short jail stays. Each time, Leo felt sorry for Nick's young family, and he bailed him out. When he questioned Nick about using drugs, Nick flatly denied he had a problem.

Nick's young wife told Leo and Sharon that she and the children were leaving Nick. Her husband was hooked with a $250-per-day cocaine habit. Often there was no food in the house. Nick, not wanting to do drugs alone, had tried to force her to take them, too. Nervous, bleary-eyed men were always showing up at their house for drugs. "It's not safe for us to stay with him anymore," she explained.

Soon after his wife left, Nick got a divorce and moved in with a young woman who was pregnant with his child. He went to see his dad, pleading for a job. "Please, Dad, I want to make something of my life."

So Leo reached out again and arranged for his son to manage one of his franchise restaurants. Each day, when Nick came to work, his live-in girlfriend and their baby came, too. "A pitiful trio," Leo thought to himself. He couldn't help noticing Nick's cloudy eyes and shaking hands. At twenty-four, still hooked on drugs, his son was racing on a collision course with disaster.

As daylight peeked across the horizon outside Leo's home, he finally dozed. Too soon, the aroma of coffee woke him. "Time to get up, Honey. I'm going to work early this morning," Sharon said, as she placed his cup of coffee on the bedside table and handed him the newspaper.

Leo unfolded it. Bold headlines shouted Nick's name—right after the words, "murder suspect."

Leo froze. Was this a joke? A bad dream?

He called to Sharon as she headed out the door, "I'll probably be late coming in." Tossing the paper aside, he ran to the bathroom and threw up.

Please Turn Yourself In!

"If I could get my hands on Nick right now, I might choke him to death myself!" he shouted. Looking at his own big hands, gnarled from years of hard work, he was horrified at the thought he could ever use them against his eldest son. His fury gave way to pity. Then to grief. He fell headlong across the unmade bed, sobbing uncontrollably.

"How could Nick hurt so many people who love him? His mother and me, his grandmother, his four children, the two women who have borne his children? How could he?" Leo cried.

He reached for the phone beside his bed and dialed an unlisted number Nick had given him a few weeks earlier. After the fifth ring, his son's voice came on the line.

Leo was blunt: "Nick, I'm not asking if you did or didn't murder the woman. I'm asking you to turn yourself in. The newspaper says you are wanted. Don't make the police chase you down. Turn yourself in," he urged. "I can probably come up with the bail money. I beg you, make it easier on yourself and on your mom and me."

Nick mumbled an incomprehensible response. Leo hung up and wondered if he'd done the wrong thing, offering again to bail his son out. Once more he sobbed, holding his head in tear-soaked hands. "If I don't stop crying, this pain will rip apart my insides," he told himself. He cried for another hour, until weary and desperate, he slipped to his knees to pray.

"I Choose to Forgive"

"Lord Jesus, I choose to forgive Nick. And I ask You to forgive him. I commit him and the days ahead to You. I know he is my son, no matter what happens, so help me be to him what he needs me to be—no more, no less."

Leo called Sharon to tell her the news. After the next few hours, their lives would never be the same. Nick turned himself in and was put in jail.

At his trial, Nick pleaded "no contest" to the homicide charge. Both he and his partner-in-crime received forty-five-year prison sentences.

Neither man admitted firing the shot that killed the woman when she caught them hauling out her household goods. She had confiscated the goods earlier from Nick's partner as payment for drugs, and they'd tried to get them back. She fired the first two shots. High on drugs, the two men retaliated.

Love Covers a Multitude of Sins

Leo struggled with bouts of guilt and depression over his son's crime. Where had he failed as a father? He and Sharon reared their sons in a Christian home from the time they were small. Hindsight seemed so clear! He wished he had separated Nick from his wild friends when he was in the seventh grade. Or that he had said no when he wanted to marry so young. Or that he had let Nick stay in jail until he'd come to grips with his need to be drug-free.

Like many modern parents, Leo and Sharon refused to recognize their son could be involved with drugs. In junior high school, when Nick's friends were rude, disobedient, and untrustworthy—something foreign to their own family's way of life—they failed to see the problem.

Now as they talked, Leo and Sharon admitted their mistakes. They realized they couldn't wallow in the past but had to take responsibility for their errors and move ahead by asking God's forgiveness. They made a deliberate decision to forgive Nick, determining that his crime would never separate him from their love.

Leo visited Nick in jail. He looked him square in the face and said, "I forgive you, Son."

Sharon, not yet emotionally strong enough to see her son behind bars, wrote a letter. "Nick, I forgive you for all the suffering your drug problem has caused us. I love you. Please forgive me for not being a better mother to you."

Later Sharon told me, "As parents and Christians, our love for our children can be like a big blanket of forgiveness to spread over the hurt; love covers a multitude of sins."

Forgiveness Is A Choice

Forgiveness—possible? Yes! Easy? No!

How do Christian parents forgive a drug-addicted child when he drags himself, his parents, and the rest of the family through dangerous, destructive, and humiliating situations? Three mothers of children once addicted to drugs offer insights from their personal journeys to forgiveness.

Ellen, the mother of a son once a user and a dealer, said, "It has been easier for me to forgive because I realize how much God has forgiven me. But my husband, an unbeliever, still has a hard time forgiving. He's a strong person and believes anyone can get off drugs or alcohol just by determination and will power. I know it needs to be done through the enabling power of the Lord."

Kay, whose son is imprisoned for a murder conviction, shared her insight: "Forgiveness is a choice; it is not a feeling. I asked God for the needed heart-change in me. Yet I had to say aloud over and over, 'I forgive my son; I forgive my son.' I also had to forgive his undesirable friends for their influence on him, when I wanted to blame them."

While these parents chose to forgive their sons, they admitted they had other gut-level emotions to deal with. "I hated his weakness in turning to drugs as an escape valve," Ellen admitted. "It's easier to take drugs than face reality. He obviously didn't feel his parents—or even God—could meet his needs. He became a drug dealer to support his habit. He'd go three to four months without a snort, then he'd almost kill himself on a drug binge."

Although her son is off drugs, Ellen continues to pray this prayer for her son: "Father, confront him with Jesus; let there be a repentance toward the ones he has pierced—his Lord and his family."

When Lucinda first learned her son Derek had been arrested for kidnapping, she went into a denial period. *Her* son would never behave like a criminal and commit a crime! When her husband told her what he'd learned from the police, she moved beyond denial and accepted that he was guilty.

Initially, Lucinda tried to blame any other person besides Derek—his friends for their bad influence, her husband for his busyness, herself for her community involvements. Finally, she acknowledged that her son, of his own free will, chose to break the law. He was responsible for his own behavior. In admitting that, she saw what was inside her own heart—unforgiveness.

Her journey to forgiveness began when she humbled herself and asked God's forgiveness for her failure as a mother. Every time she remembered an incident in which she had failed Derek, she expressed her feelings of inadequacy and her regrets. She asked the Lord to forgive her son and his accomplices in crime. She also asked her husband to forgive her for shifting blame onto him.

After Derek served four years of his fifteen-year sentence, he was released on probation and lived at home again. Finding a job was difficult, and he often showed his despondency by staying in bed for hours during the day. Soon, to his parents' dismay, he moved in with his girlfriend. After some time, he found a job and decided to get married.

Lucinda and her husband attended the wedding. In the following weeks, their relationship with Derek grew stronger. "We really had to walk in forgiveness when he was living with his girlfriend," she told me. "Thank the Lord, he did not go back into the drug culture. Things are much better between us now that he's married and responsible for a wife. Of course, we continue to pray that Derek and his wife will commit their lives to God."

These mothers—Ellen, Kay, and Lucinda—can look back and see how God has used their heartache to enable them to help others. Parents whose children are putting them through the treadmill of hurt find compassion and comfort from others who can relate to their problems.

Should a drug-addicted child remain at home? Many parents struggle with this question. One mother said, "Sometimes, as mothers, we have to assent to things we don't condone, such as allowing a child to remain at home even when we know he is sneaking around getting drugs—especially if having him stay is our husband's decision."

I know parents who have asked their drug- or alcohol-problem child to leave because younger children in the home were being adversely affected. Others allow them to stay in an effort to help them overcome their addiction.

Single Parent Struggle

Dot, a midwestern working mom and single parent, has successfully come through her ordeal with a heavily addicted son who was much too young to be asked to leave home. Her husband abandoned the family to marry his secretary when Max was only eight years old. Two years later, devastated by his father's leaving, Max started smoking marijuana with his friends. By eighth grade, he was heavily into both drugs and alcohol, often stealing from his mother's purse to buy them.

"At first I was naive, protecting my own heart," Dot says. "I chose to ignore and deny the obvious symptoms of drug use: secretive phone calls, lots of kids I'd never met going in and out of our home, the disappearance of dozens of sandwich baggies, money missing from my purse, numerous talks with teachers and school officials about his behavior, catching him in lies. . . .

"I had to work to support the family, so I couldn't always be home when Max came in from school," she related. "I worked for a Christian organization, and friends there gave me needed prayer support. Often, I felt as if my home had been invaded by a burglar. Eventually, I could not endure any more, and I started looking for a place to send Max for help."

Once, when Max overdosed, he was so sure he was going to die that he checked into a treatment center for four months. When he was released, he had a couple of "slips" which made him realize all his old friends had to go.

Earlier, Max had viewed his mother as an interfering old lady who intruded in his life with advice and prayers. Now, fully rehabilitated, he is grateful she loved him enough to reach out and help him. "We had a lot of forgiving to do, but with God's help we have talked through our hurts," she said.

As a growing Christian, Max encourages other young people to stay away from drugs by speaking to groups and on radio talk shows. He is twenty-one and has been free of drugs and alcohol for five years.

The Futility of Anger

Anger—intense anger Dolores didn't know she was capable of harboring—boiled to the explosion point one day. She discovered her thirteen-year-old Willie smoking marijuana with his friends in the woods behind their house. She grabbed him by the ear, jerked him up, and propelled him along the path toward home. "Why are you doing this to me?" she yelled, shaking with rage. He didn't bother to answer.

Alarmed by her unbridled anger toward her son, Dolores dug through Scripture until she found something to help bring her anger under control. A verse in James became her lifeline:

> "Be quick to listen, slow to speak and slow to become angry, for man's anger does not bring about the righteous life that God desires." (James 1:19,20).

She smiled as she shared her experience with me. "I realized anger was a useless indulgence," she said. "My job was to love Willie and to try to keep communcation with him. Every time I'd get angry, I'd pray, 'Lord, I know my anger will not make a righteous man out of my son. Only Your power can do that.'"

First-Aid Book

Willie got an after-school job, then bought a big black motor-cycle. Many nights, he stayed out long past curfew. Dolores would wake up in a cold sweat, imagining his bloody body entangled in a wreckage in some roadside ditch. Days passed when she wondered if there was any hope at all for Willie.

"I finally confessed that I was a poor mother, and I asked Jesus to forgive me," she told me. "That was primary to my being able to forgive Willie for being such a difficult son. Even at that, my forgiveness of him had to be renewed every single day."

For five long years, Dolores tried to communicate with Willie without seeing much improvement. During that time, the Lord had given her an incredible idea: She made herself a "first-aid book" containing promises from the Bible which she read over and over until a tiny spark of hope was rekindled in her heart. God's promises were all she had to cling to when she knew Willie was still smoking marijuana behind her back.

Forgiveness Began a New Work

Dolores and her husband made a significant decision—to pull back from Willie and not reach out to him, to wait for him to come to them. They never stopped praying for him.

One spring afternoon just after his twentieth birthday, Willie decided to accompany his parents to his sister's college graduation. When they got home that evening, Willie fell on his mother's shoulder, crying for no apparent reason. Her husband came in, and together they held Willie while he sobbed his heart out. "I've been feeling lonely and abandoned lately, Mom," he confessed. "I don't like living like this."

Forgiveness began a new work in all their hearts, but old hurts and past mistakes had to be dealt with. "Mom, I remember a time when you said you hated me," Willie said to Dolores a few days later.

"I never hated you, and I never said that," she answered, horrified.

"Little by little Satan's work in planting lies in Willie's mind was uncovered," she told me. "His dad and I prayed for him to be set free, which we could not have done had we not released our anger and fully forgiven him. I lost count of the times I said to him, 'Willie, I love you. I forgive you. I'm available anytime you want to talk.' "

Working hard to keep that commitment, Dolores would sit and listen as Willie shared about school, his dog, girls, or his job. They took long walks in the woods together, philosophizing about life. When she felt the time was right, she talked with him about God. She and her husband talked honestly with him about their mistakes and disappointments.

There was no instant cure for Willie. Over the next four years he was gradually delivered from marijuana, alcohol, and chewing tobacco. For nine years, his parents had been on a rollercoaster with their son—praying, forgiving, praying, forgiving, praying some more. Today Willie is living close to the Lord, and

Dolores says he is a joy to be around. He even has a part-time prison ministry.

"My hope was not in my own authority," she says, looking back. "So many times in the past, my anger had come from believing I had to be an enforcer and feeling I had failed. Nor was my hope in counselors, reform schools, or hospitals, though God can certainly use them. My confidence was in God Himself. His kindness brought Willie to repentance" (see Romans 2:4).

Why They Take Drugs

"The great majority of drug-using children make their initial decision to try a drug between their twelfth and sixteenth years." [4] Why do they start? Researchers say teens want to "belong to the group" and are more interested in peer-group acceptance than parental or adult approval. [5]

"Five reasons for youngsters giving in to drugs are *pressure, escape, availability, curiosity, and emptiness,*" says Jay Strack. [6]

A former drug-abuser who was rescued from an alcohol-shattered family and is now a pastor, Strack recommends these instructions when counseling teens with drug or alcohol problems:

1. Be approachable and available. Encourage the young person to face his problem honestly. Encourage him to talk about pent-up feelings.
2. Encourage him to accept responsibility in this problem. He is accountable for his own behavior.
3. Ask if he wants to be healed. Is he willing to give up the sin?
4. Listen to him.
5. Don't react with shock or disgust.
6. Get on his level and don't blow up. Let your child know you are upset because you love him and are concerned about his direction in life. (Don't be more embarrassed about your failure than concerned about the condition of the child.)
7. Don't betray confidences.
8. Be positive; offer hope.

9. Remind the teenager there are no quick solutions.
10. Encourage goal setting; explain that God offers an abundant, exciting life (John 10:10).
11. Ask the Holy Spirit for guidance and strength; use the Bible for counseling.
12. Find out what programs are available, but don't act as if you are an authority if you aren't.
13. Count the cost of counseling. Be sure to lead the person to Jesus and point out that He can forgive sins and take away guilt. Challenge the person to be a victor, no longer a victim of drugs or alcohol. [7]

Gaining the Victory

Leo, whose son Nick is still in prison for his drug-related homicide, told me, "No one can function properly when under the influence of drugs. Only God can set such a person free. My son embarrassed and hurt us, but I have embarrassed and hurt my heavenly Father, too. He still loves and forgives me. Could I do any less with my own son? Jesus said if I pray to be forgiven, I must forgive others. As a Christian, I have no other choice. I have learned a whole new dimension of love and forgiveness through our horrible ordeal."

Max's mother, Dot, says, "Other parents dealing with a drug-dependent child must keep praying and trusting God to intervene and restore. The very thing the enemy meant for destruction, God will use for His glory. I've got my sweet, wonderful son back, but it took years to get to this place."

Christian parents I spoke with who have forgiven their chemically-addicted children related the steps they took to gain victory:
1. Acknowledge your failure as parents.
2. Ask God to forgive you.
3. Ask God to forgive your child.

4. Regardless of how much he's hurt you, give your child love and support without making excuses for his sin.
5. Keep praying and believing God will turn your child around.
6. Remember, nothing is impossible with God!

Prayer

Lord God of Hosts, You are the great Deliverer. We ask You to move mightily on behalf of our son/daughter, _____. Deliver him/her from evil. Show him/her a way of escape. Convict him/her of this destructive sin that hurts You so greatly. Father, I am reminding You that the seed of the righteous shall be delivered, and I thank You that the work of the enemy in this child's life is broken, in Jesus' name.

I am righteous because of the blood of Jesus, and my child is my seed. So Lord, deliver him/her and bring about Your good and right and perfect plan for his/her life.

Thank You that You know the plans You have for _____'s future—plans for his/her good, not for calamity. I praise and thank You in advance for the way You will move to save and restore my child, because it is not Your will that any should perish, but that all shall come to repentance. Lord, Your word says nothing is impossible for You; I'm standing on that promise! In Jesus' name, Amen. (Prayer based on 1 John 1:7; Proverbs 11:21, KJV; Jeremiah 29:11; 2 Peter 3:9; Luke 1:37.)

Twelve

Forgiving In-Law Children

Picture this scene: An older woman pulls up in front of her daughter's house in a taxi. As she's paying her fare, her son-in-law rushes down the walk to help carry in her suitcase. The driver hops to the trunk and pulls out four more bags and the son-in-law gulps and says, "But I thought you were just staying for the weekend!"

Mother-in-law jokes make their point: relationships between child-in-law and a parent-in-law are not easy. In fact, they are often strained—fraught with misunderstanding and resentment.

Merging two families isn't easy. In the best of circumstances, our expectations of each other, our prejudices, our human failings occasionally sabotage family relationships.

Misunderstandings and Hurt Feelings

Differences often crop up between parents and their children's mates. Here are a few of the grievances I've heard:

151

- A son-in-law who allows his wife to visit her parents only every two years, even when a free plane ticket is offered.
- A daughter-in-law who insists on spending all the holidays with her family, never with his.
- A daughter-in-law who never invites her husband's parents for a meal, though they frequently invite her and their son for dinner.
- A son-in-law who insists on handling the finances, including his wife's earnings, and squanders the money on his own selfish interests.
- A son-in-law who accepts a down-payment on a house from his wife's parents but shows no gratitude for the gift.
- A daughter-in-law or son-in-law who won't allow their spouse any contact with their family or friends.
- A son-in-law or daughter-in-law who influences his/her spouse to stop attending church.

Young people these days often meet their mates after leaving for college or finding a job, so the in-law child may come from a totally different background than that of the family back home. That usually calls for grace and forbearance for both sets of parents.

In Bible times, families were generally more closely knit than in today's western cultures, and parents had a strong say-so in their child's choice of a mate. Also, since a girl often married at an early age and moved either nearby or in with her husband's family, her mother-in-law customarily continued the training her own mother started. As a result, a loving and strong bond usually developed between these two, as illustrated when Naomi referred to her widowed daughter-in-law, Ruth, as "my daughter." [1]

Let's reflect a moment on Naomi and Ruth's special relationship.

Biblical In-Laws, Naomi and Ruth
When famine hit Bethlehem, Naomi's Hebrew husband

Elimelech moved his family to Moab where food was more plentiful. Their two sons married Moabite girls, Orpah and Ruth (see Ruth chapter 1).

Problem: Moabites were foreigners to the Jews and, while marriage to Moabite women was not forbidden, any sons of such marriages were excluded, to the tenth generation, from entering the assembly of the Lord (see Deuteronomy 23:2,3).

We are not told what resentments Naomi may have felt toward her sons for marrying aliens or toward the foreign daughters-in-law. Because of the serious implications, we can reasonably assume she must have struggled with it. The very close bond between Naomi and Ruth leads us to believe Naomi came to a position of forgiveness.

After the death of her husband and her two sons, Naomi decided to return to Bethlehem. Ruth's attachment is apparent in her powerful declaration, "Where you go I will go, and where you stay I will stay. Your people will be my people and your God my God" (Ruth 1:16).

A Gentile committed herself to her Jewish mother-in-law and to the God of the Jews. Following through that commitment by scrupulous obedience to Naomi's guidance resulted in her marriage to Boaz. When their son Obed was born, friends said to Naomi, "Your daughter-in-law, who loves you and who is better to you than seven sons, has given him birth" (Ruth 4:15).

What a tribute! To have seven sons would be the epitome of a Hebrew family blessing; to have Ruth as a daughter-in-law was judged to be the equivalent! The discrimination practiced against the offspring of a Moabitess must have been forgotten, because among Obed's descendants were King David and our Lord Jesus Christ Himself.

The prophet Micah described a strife-torn family as one in which a daughter rises up against her mother, and a daughter-in-law against her mother-in-law (see Micah 7:6). God's answer to strife, or potential strife, is love and forgiveness. The story of

Naomi and Ruth is a glorious example of covenantal love between in-laws. We see God's love at work. Ruth was betrothed to Boaz, her kinsman-redeemer; and Naomi's emptiness turned to fulness. Probability: Forgiveness helped make it all possible.

Modern Mother-In-Law

Frankie, the keynote speaker at a large Christian women's meeting, started to tell the story of her son's recent miraculous healing when she paused and motioned for a woman on the front row to come to the platform.

"I want to introduce my wonderful daughter-in-law, Kathryn," she said with pride. "She has been a faithful wife who stood by my son during his critical illness, and I greatly appreciate her."

The young woman held her head a bit higher and threw her mother-in-law one of the biggest Texas grins I'd ever seen. I watched, puzzled, as Kathryn returned to her seat.

I knew the two of them had not had a close relationship. In fact, they were often worlds apart. Kathryn had met Frankie's son Ralph at the beach soon after he'd divorced his first wife, and they rushed into a marriage that Frankie and her husband openly opposed.

"What prompted you to recognize Kathryn like that?" I asked Frankie afterwards. "I thought you'd had a problem accepting her, especially since you wanted your son to marry a Christian."

"While preparing my speech, God dealt with me about my judgmental attitude toward Kathryn," Frankie admitted. "Remember how I used to complain about her? When He pointed out my sin, I knew I was guilty; I had judged her many times. I asked the Lord to forgive me, and I made a decision to forgive Kathryn. The Lord wanted me to recognize her publicly to affirm her for some good, positive quality."

From that day on, Frankie and her daughter-in-law enjoyed a more harmonious relationship than many mothers and daughters do. The secret? First, Frankie responded to the Holy Spirit's nudge; she recognized her judgmental attitude and forgave Kathryn. She decided to accent the positive instead of dwelling on the negative. Her daughter-in-law has now given her heart to the Lord.

Major on Good Qualities

Soon after that meeting, I visited Norma, a friend in another state. As we sipped herb tea at her kitchen table, she told me how difficult it was to accept her three young daughters-in-law. All three lived nearby, so she couldn't avoid noticing their weak characteristics. One was always late; another watched too many soap operas; another was a "mama's baby," always running home when she got miffed.

I shared my friend Frankie's experience and how she now looks for "plus" traits in her daughters-in-law. "Do you feel you need to forgive your sons' wives?" I asked. "Maybe you should thank God for some of their good qualities and commend them for those things."

Norma was open to the idea. Before we'd finished our tea, she bowed her head, forgave each daughter-in-law, and thanked God for these special young women her sons had married.

In the following weeks, Norma continued to thank Him for her daughters-in-law, for the virtuous attributes. They are good cooks and homemakers. They love their husbands and try to cooperate with their plans to go camping, hunting and fishing. Two of the three attend church on Sundays. All three had a lot of positive traits. She simply needed to look for them.

Norma phoned a few months later, ecstatic about the improved relationships with her daughters-in-law. Since that day we prayed in her kitchen, they began sensing her acceptance. Could it be that her willingness to forgive had set them free? Or that forgiveness made it possible for her to see sterling qualities God is still refining?

Forgive God, Too

A woman who heard me speak about our need to forgive our children asked afterward, "Must we forgive sons-in-law, too?"

"Yes, of course, when that's needed," I answered the intense woman.

"You don't understand," she said with anguish written on her face. "My son-in-law recently burned down the new million-dollar church I attend. It is so embarrassing—it has been head-line news all over our state. If he goes to prison, I'll probably have to take care of my daughter and their children. It's hard to forgive him."

As we prayed, it became apparent that she'd just touched the tip of the iceberg. Her real feelings were against God; she blamed Him that her daughter had married a man she secretly considered to be a bum. Why hadn't He protected her daughter from this terrible mistake?

"Do you think you need to forgive God?" I asked.

The idea registered. "Yes...yes...that's it! Oh God, I blamed You," she cried. "I forgive You. My daughter made her own choice. Please forgive me, Lord."

As she continued praying aloud, she forgave her daughter for disappointing her and forgave her son-in-law as well. She asked for forgiveness for her judgmental attitude. A sense of relief swept over her as she relinquished the "whole package" into the Lord's hands.

"There, it's done!" she declared. "He's forgiven, and I'm forgiven. And I trust God with the future." Of course, the road ahead of her is still difficult because of the seriousness of her son-in-law's crime. But now she can walk that road with God's strength and enablement, without the additional burden of bitterness and unforgiveness.

When They Marry An Unbeliever

Esther's strikingly beautiful twenty-year-old daughter Diane was high on drugs the afternoon the motorcycle on which she was a passenger sped out of control. It crashed, throwing Diane, spinning like a baseball, into a cement wall. Her back was broken. She was a paraplegic.

Diane had been a professing Christian. After her paralysis, she did a complete turn around and rebelled against God. During her treatment at a rehabilitation center, she fell in love with Tim, an attendant there. She made plans to marry him, though her parents tried their best to dissuade her.

"Here she was—paralyzed, confined forever to a wheel-chair, and running from God—insisting she was going to marry a non-Christian," Esther shared with me one evening after a service at her church. "My heart was broken. What happened to all those prayers I'd prayed for her to have a Christian husband?"

Subconsciously, Esther blamed this older man for "stealing" her daughter. "I asked myself how I could ever love him, let alone forgive him," she told me.

Feeling this way, Esther and her husband did not attend Diane's wedding. Five years later, when Diane gave birth to her "miracle daughter," she evidenced an overwhelming desire to mend the broken relationship with her parents.

"When she phoned, we would always be cheerful, helpful, and loving," Esther related. "But our relationship with Diane's husband was still touchy at best. We felt he was aloof, a stranger, untouchable, and trying to protect Diane from us."

One morning, as Esther was talking to God, she blurted out her feelings about her disappointments in her son-in-law. When I admitted my honest reaction, the Lord showed me the unforgiveness that was in my heart," she said. "I saw it! And I asked for His forgiveness. Tim probably had no concerned Christians praying for him. Overwhelmed with compassion rather than anger, I determined to "stand in the gap" in prayer until he came to know the Lord Jesus.

"You can't pray for someone as hard as I was praying for Tim and not forgive. God wouldn't have heard my prayers had I remained clogged with the garbage of unforgiveness."

The next step for Esther was to forgive Diane for marrying Tim against her wishes. "After that, my letters and phone calls to her became more frequent, and our relationship improved," she said with a smile. "Then one day Diane called with marvelous news. She had come back to the Lord! She asked me to forgive her for all her rebellious years and to join her in praying for Tim to become a Christian. She didn't know I had been doing that for a long, long time. Now we are prayer partners and closer than we've ever been."

Esther sees a softening in her son-in-law. He allows Diane to take their little girl to church. She is believing that soon all three of them will attend church together and that Tim will commit his life to the Lord.

Another Culture

When your child marries someone from another culture, you may have an especially difficult time understanding your in-law child, as Belle, a recent widow, experienced.

Her son Kirk married Lu, an oriental divorcee, when he was with the Air Force in Hawaii twelve years ago. While living in Germany and Las Vegas, their marriage was relatively stable because they enjoyed the company of many military couples like themselves. When Kirk left the military and moved to Florida, his wife discovered a whole community of war refugees from her country. As Lu spent more and more of her nights playing cards and gambling with this group of people, tension built in their marriage.

Whenever a feud breaks out between Lu and Kirk, their six-year-old daughter Akiko is sent to Grandma Belle's. Sometimes she stays overnight; sometimes she stays several days. On occasion, when Lu is quarreling with Kirk, she herself may come and stay at Belle's home, bringing with her her deep-seated fears of evil spirits lurking in the dark, her ancestor worship, and her belief in reincarnation. Some of her unusual habits are based on superstition; some come from fears she picked up during the war when she was the only member of her immediate family to survive.

Accept Them As They Are

Belle decided long ago she wouldn't tell her children how to live; she would accept them and their spouses just as they are, even when she doesn't approve of their ways.

Recently, Kirk's best friend died of cancer. When Kirk went to help the friend's wife straighten out her legal papers and to do some house repairs, Lu became jealous. In a fit of rage, she threw Kirk's clothes out, gathered up her jewelry, and ran screaming into Belle's house to tell her how awful her son was. "I'm leaving him, and I've got my jewelry to sell for money to survive on," she shouted.

After a brief chase down the driveway, Belle grabbed her arm and spun the tiny woman around. She looked her in the eye and said, "Lu, I'm the only mother you have to love you. Stop this foolishness. Kirk is not interested in that widow. He only wants to help her. He'd want his best friend to do the same for you, wouldn't he?"

Lu broke into sobs. She agreed to take Akiko, go home, and return Kirk's clothes.

They are now putting their marriage back together. Kirk, though innocent of any wrongdoing concerning the widow, asked Lu to forgive him.

"Now that I've accepted Lu as she is, it makes forgiving a lot easier," Belle confided to me. "Because of cultural differences, I still find it hard to understand some of her ways; but I am committed to be a loving mother-in-law to her."

Teach Younger Wives

Ever watch a mother cat or dog defend her babies? Nature's example is graphic: you touch my offspring, and you deal with me. In much the same way, human parents instinctively bristle when their child is "attacked." Such a response in an in-law situation has the potential for torpedoing a relationship. There's another way around this problem, as my friend Judy discovered when her daughter-in-law Toni kept criticizing her son.

Instead of silently brewing over the attacks, Judy directly, but gently, challenged her son's wife. "Don't you ever do anything wrong?" she asked. "I know I'm lacking in many areas of my life. It's self-righteous for us to exalt ourselves above our husbands."

I was surprised at the openness in the relationship. "Doesn't she resent your being so direct?" I asked.

"No, not really," Judy answered. "We have a healthy relationship. She allows me to help her work on areas where she needs improvement, but I only do it when I see she is out of line with God's standard. We read the Bible together to find an answer to whatever is troubling her. The apostle Paul told the older women to train the younger women to love their husbands and children. I try to do that since Toni doesn't have her own mom now."

"You two have an unusual relationship," I remarked.

"Maybe so. We don't ignore our differences; we talk them out, either by phone or person-to-person," Judy said. "I forgive her every time a hurtful situation comes up. If she keeps on talking against my son, I will remind her that the Bible says, 'Bear with each other and forgive whatever grievances you have against one another. Forgive as the Lord forgave you" (Col. 3:13).

"I Long to Hold My Grandson"

On one of my speaking trips, I stayed in the home of Lydia, a widow whose son was kidnapped and murdered on his way to work a few years ago. Her former daughter-in-law won't let her see her grandson, though they live in a neighboring town. Naturally, her heart aches.

"Forgive her? Yes, I've forgiven her, and I pray for her every day," she said sadly. "But I long to hold my grandson. He looks so much like my son, and it would give me comfort to have him visit me, if only once a year. All my letters and packages to him are returned. But that doesn't erase the fact that he is my grandson. Maybe someday, when he is older, he'll find a way to come and see me."

Mothers like Lydia are not isolated cases. There are hundreds of mothers whose former in-law children deny their offspring the privilege of knowing grandmother and granddad, creating yet another need for grandparents for forgive and continue praying for God's intervention. Someday, I hope to hear that Lydia's prayers have been answered.

Love Never Fails

"Love never fails," Paul wrote to the Corinthians. "These three remain: faith, hope and love. But the greatest of these is love" (1 Cor. 13:8,13). Getting along with in-law children is smoother sailing when we exhibit all three.

I was visiting my friend Bettye, enjoying pumpkin pie and coffee, right after her son and family had left from a Thanksgiving visit.

"It would be natural for me to get upset," she said, sharing about her relationship with her daughter-in-law. "She's started taking my grandson to a religious group that my husband and I don't approve of. When I start to react, the Lord reminds me, 'You just love her!' "

"Is that hard to do?" I asked.

"Sometimes it is," she said, nodding. "But when I draw her in as a part of my treasured family and treat her in a loving way, she responds with warmth and tenderness. She's my son's wife and the mother of my grandchildren, so I'm trusting the Lord and keeping my mouth shut about her false religion. She knows that we believe Jesus Christ is the Son of God and the only way to obtain salvation."

Bettye stopped to refill my coffee cup, then continued. "At first, I was hurt that she is exposing my young grandson to her false teaching. But I have been able to forgive her. God requires from me faith, hope, and love. That's what I'm counting on to see me through. Love never fails; it always wins!"

I believe Bettye is right. She's found an unbeatable solution to to in-law problems.

Prayer

Father, I confess to You it is often hard to love my in-law child, _____. Forgive me for judging him/her and for thinking he/she isn't good enough or smart enough or prosperous enough to be a part of our family. Lord, I forgive my child for disappointing me in his/her choice for a mate. Help me be a good in-law parent who shows unconditional love to my adult child and his/her spouse, as well as to my grandchild(ren). Help me to be loving and caring without becoming meddlesome and to be faithful to encourage them and to pray for them. In Jesus' name I ask, Amen.

Thirteen

When Your Children Disappoint You

She wore what looked like a permanent frown. The sad-faced woman across the cafeteria table from me was obviously burdened with disappointment and worry. "I have a teenage son I just can't forgive," she blurted as we ate lunch together following the women's meeting where I had just spoken.

"Out of seven pregnancies, only three of my children lived. This boy causes me so much embarrassment, pain, worry, and expense that I have often asked God why he lived instead of one of my precious babies who died." My heart ached for her as she continued to air her grievances against her son.

"The slammed doors, the harsh words, the rebellion—it's enough to make me turn in my mother's badge! I want to forgive him; I'm struggling to do it; but I can't," she said emphatically.

I gently urged her to release her anger and frustration to the Lord and to *choose* to forgive her son. "If you take that step as an act of your will, God will help you and will renew your love for this boy."

This mother faced the challenge and opportunity to shower love and acceptance on a special son who desperately needed it. But her hurt immobilized her. "I just can't do it," she insisted, shaking her head in hopelessness.

The pain and anger she'd buried blinded her from seeing her need to forgive her son. Until she could perceive this, the door to healing and reconciliation would remain closed. "Oh, Lord, help her," I prayed.

Bound to Disappoint

Children are bound to disappoint you. It goes with the territory—a basic fact of parenting. Inevitably, parents have hopes and expectations for their children—high hopes that they will marry "well," choose the "right" career, live their lives according to "good" standards. When parents' fantasies don't materialize, the parents feel let down—in a word, *disappointed.*

My friends Hanna and Bill were disappointed in their son Charlie who hadn't had a job in a year. They were driving to their Florida vacation cottage, discussing the problem, when Hanna said, "Honey, maybe our expectations for Charlie are too high . . . maybe we want him to excel because of our own pride. He likes to work with his hands. He's not suited to working at a bank or an office the way you are."

"I think you're right," Bill answered, nodding his head. "I've thought about this a lot over the past year. Let's relinquish this to the Lord."

Right there in the car, they prayed aloud and released Charlie to the Lord, asking God to work His will in their son. The next week, he got a job working outdoors with his hands.

Hanna told me about it later when we were sitting on the porch of their vacation cottage, watching her husband and son fish in the bay.

"We decided we couldn't play God in Charlie's life anymore," she said. "We are concerned about his financial situation. While he was off work that year he built a log home for his family, but he needed an income. When we took our hands off the situation, in a sense we forgave him for disappointing us; then God provided the job he needed. Now Bill and I both enjoy a wonderful relationship with our son."

"Forgive the Trivial"

Forgiveness is available for *every* problem. God doesn't want us to save up for "the biggies." Sometimes parents dismiss feelings or ignore what seems trivial, not realizing that even small things can develop into serious relational roadblocks. Consider, for instance, a few of the comments I've heard from mothers who resented their new babies:

> "I'm still overweight after my pregnancy. . . I haven't been able to sleep three hours straight for weeks, getting up nights with this crying baby.. . . This was an unplanned pregnancy and I'm too old to be a mother. . . My husband and I have no time alone now that we have a house full of kids. I have no identity except as a mother. . . ." One dared to confess to me, "Frankly, I'm disappointed in my child. He's not cute or bright or even a good baby."

These and countless other complaints come from mothers who find themselves overwhelmed in their parental role. A sense of humor and a fresh perspective can help. Try imagining how God must feel with some of His kids! After all, we have a God who relates to our disappointments and, in His compassion, stands ready to forgive our inadequacies and redeem our mistakes.

Forgiveness: Oft-Repeated Necessity

"I wasn't sure when my children's misbehavior stopped being

a normal part of childhood that required correction and started being a catalyst for my temper," wrote Debbie Hedstrom. "My kids did so many things that angered me: Jim's arguing, Jerry's tattling, Julie's emotional outbursts, and Janet's whining."

At first, Debbie dismissed her flare-ups as a temporary result of cranky kids. Later, she faced the fact that she dreaded their arrival home from school. When she prayed about it, the Lord showed her she had never forgiven her children.

"How had I missed the obvious?" she asked. "Though I'd asked God to forgive me, I hadn't sought help in forgiving my children's faults. No wonder the first offense of the morning made me mad.

"I wanted to get rid of my children's yesterdays, so I gave God the arguing, tattling, outbursts, and whining. I asked Him to help me forgive as He does—with nothing left clinging. But immediately I thought, *I'm going to have to do this a thousand times before my kids are grown!*

This wise mother concluded, "Daily relationships make forgiveness an often repeated necessity, without limits. Although I've learned about forgiveness and gotten below the surface of its pat phrases, it hasn't taken away all the problems with my children. But I don't have to grope for answers when I struggle. I know the power of forgiveness." [1]

Why Have You Treated Us Like This?

Does it offer you any comfort to know that Jesus' mother was anxious about Him? Maybe disappointed? Remember when He was twelve years old and the family was returning home after spending some days at the Feast of Passover in Jerusalem? They assumed He was in their caravan, but when they began looking for Him among their acquaintances, He was missing. Returning to Jerusalem, they began an all-out search.

They found Him, of all places, in the temple, sitting among the teachers, asking questions and listening. Mary had a question for Him—one which mothers have asked through the centuries. "Son, why have you treated us like this?" (Luke 2:48).

How many of us have lain awake into the wee hours of the morning, waiting for our children to come home?

One summer, my two older children borrowed my car to drive to an out-of-state worship congress. "We'll be home by one in the morning at the latest," they promised.

One o'clock came and went; I lay awake all night waiting and praying. By five a.m., I couldn't stand the strain any longer. My husband made phone calls until he found them. "We got too sleepy to drive," Quinett explained, "so we stopped to sleep for awhile. It was so late we didn't want to call and wake you up." I was torn between being thankful they were alive and well and being perturbed over my lost sleep. Even "good Christian kids" give parents moments of anxiety and opportunities to keep forgiving.

Unique Individuals

Many parents have difficulty recognizing their children as unique gifts from God. We tend to want to mold them into careers we like or see them marry to "better themselves" or we push them to fulfill dreams we once dreamed for ourselves. The Bible, however, tells us each child has an individual bent or talent:

> "Train up a child in the way he should go (and in keeping with his individual gift or bent), and when he is old he will not depart from it" (Prov. 22:6 TAB).

God has a plan and pattern for every person's life, including our children's lives. Our role as Christian parents necessitates relinquishing our children so they might find God's will for their lives and that He might accomplish His will in them.

Offering Our Children to God

I recently heard Bible teacher Jean Norment say, "Worship is the voluntary sacrifice of everything I value most. Abraham was offering not only Isaac in sacrifice, he was offering everything he owned. Once a man offers his best, he's given everything else."

Think about Abraham's willingness to give up Isaac, the son embodying all the promises God made to Abraham. This special son, Abraham's own seed, was to inherit all God had promised. Yet Scripture tells us clearly:

> "By faith Abraham, when God tested him, offered Isaac as a sacrifice. He who had received the promises was about to sacrifice his one and only son, even though God had said to him, 'It is through Isaac that your offspring will be reckoned.' Abraham reasoned that God could raise the dead, and figuratively speaking, he did receive Isaac back from death" (Heb. 11:17–19).

Are we willing to offer our children back to God, as Abraham was willing to sacrifice his only son? Can we relinquish our disappointments in them, our unreasonable expectations for them?

Disabled Children and Parents' Anger

Mental retardation and/or learning and physical disabilities are adversities millions of parents must face. According to the Association of Retarded Citizens, retardation occurs in one of every ten families. The association estimates that more than six million people in the United States have some level of mental retardation. [2]

Corine, a lawyer's wife with seven children, knows the reality of those statistics. Her daughter Betina was born mentally disabled. Corine was one disappointed and angry mother—angry at God.

"When Betina turned three, I decided I must accept her," she shared as we visited at a women's meeting in Denver. "I had loved her since birth; but accepting her as mine, that was a different story. I forgave God for my disappointment in Him, I forgave Betina for disappointing me, and I accepted her as my own."

Coping with Betina has not gotten easier. She now has the body of an adult but the mind of a child. Currently, she is obsessed with marriage. Her younger sister is planning a wedding, and Betina fantasizes about a handsome young man who lives nearby. When she sees him with his girlfriend, she throws a temper tantrum. One day, in a fit of jealousy, she smashed the front window of his home.

"Such situations are embarrassing ," Corine said, "and I have to struggle against anger. I have to stop it the minute it surfaces or it would give way to unforgiveness."

Setting the Example

Whenever she loses her patience and says something that upsets Betina, Corine immediately says, "Oh, darling, I'm sorry. Will you forgive me?"

Sometimes Betina stares at her and says, "No, today I will not forgive you."

"But Bet, if you love Mother, you have to forgive," Corine responds. "Remember, Jesus requires you to forgive me and me to forgive you. We can't do anything else until we forgive, so let's sit down and have some tea and forgive, okay?"

It sounds easy, but it isn't. Sometimes Betina argues for hours, "No, Mom, I will not forgive." Over and over, Corine prays for patience, knowing she must set the example for her special daughter.

God has a purpose for Betina, and Corine's trusting Him to bring glory from her life. She is trying to teach Betina that getting married is not the ultimate success in life. "Betina loves the Lord and has a personal relationship with Him. I want her to see that no one else can love her as He does," she told me. "I have five sons and two daughters; and I believe God will use each of them as He did the five loaves and two fishes—to feed multitudes. Right now, some of them are in the breaking process."

If there is one statement I've heard from every parent who shared with me the heartache and disappointment of a mentally underdeveloped child, it is this: *"I have learned to walk in forgiveness daily!"*

Lost Respect

When Sue discovered her son had given his younger sister drugs, she was horrified. "I wanted to pack his bags, throw him out, and padlock the front door," she told me. "I felt he'd undermined our family, making a mockery of everything we'd taught and lived. I lost all the trust and respect I had for him."

Her husband Gene brought her back on course. "When God gave us our children, we didn't put in an order for what we wanted. These are what we got," he reminded her. "Make up your mind that they are *our* children and we're supposed to love them, no matter what. Our son needs us now."

Sue realized her husband was right. Being disappointed doesn't mean we quit loving our children. It means we have an even greater opportunity to trust for God's love and forgiveness.

Divorce Alienates

Divorce, more often than not, brings hurtful estrangement, especially if you are cut off from your child. Take Paige. After her divorce, she had dinner with her twenty-year-old son Jason to tell him goodbye before she moved out of town. Although she wrote to him numerous times, he didn't respond to her letters. She lost touch with him, assuming he'd followed his father to Oregon.

A year later, she moved back to the town where she had reared her children and remarried. One morning while grocery shopping, a former neighbor stopped to congratulate her on Jason's upcoming wedding—which, of course, Paige knew nothing about. She didn't even know Jason was in town.

"I ran out of the supermarket, drove home, and cried for three days," she told me. "I was crushed. I'd made excuses for his not writing to me, but now it seemed obvious he did not intend to include me in his life."

When she called her former minister, he said, "You mean you didn't know about the wedding? You're the mother of the groom, and of course you're welcome to attend."

Paige agonized over what to do. "I couldn't go without an invitation," she said. "If Jason wanted me there, he knew where I was. In the end, I decided to respect the distance he put between us, but it hurt.

"He was my son, a gift I'd had for twenty years; but I knew I had to let go. One day during prayer, I held my hands out in front of me, as if I were holding Jason. 'He's Yours, Lord. Please love him and guide him.' A measure of peace flowed into my heart; the hurt wasn't gone, but it no longer made me feel angry and bitter."

Paige sent a gift for Jason's wedding, with a card wishing them a full, happy life together. She signed it, "My door is always open. Love, Mother."

Although she hasn't heard from her son for four years, Paige hasn't lost hope. "I believe I will hear from him one day, because God is a restoring God," she said. "Forgive Jason? Yes, I've forgiven him just as my Lord forgave me. When the Lord brings my son back into my life, I'll be able to receive him without resentment or bitterness."

The Occult Nightmare

Most parents are naive about the strong occultic influences their children are exposed to in today's world. Young people, especially, are being drawn into occultic activity through games, rock music, drugs, and astrology. A young minister working with high school students wrote, "Kids are becoming deeply enmeshed in Dungeons and Dragons, Ouija boards, and other occult games. Standing in the wings in every town are Satanist recruiters waiting to lure them deeper. Kids are so obsessed and addicted to Ouija, it is putting them in altered mental states." [3]

A mother I will call Jolene shared her frightening experience with me.

One evening about nine o'clock, she returned from her prayer meeting to find an ambulance and police cars in front of the house. Someone had discovered her sixteen-year-old daughter Tori unconscious in the street in front of her house from a drug overdose. Doctors pumped her stomach and transferred her to the psychiatric ward for a few weeks of treatment.

"Tori had become obsessed with heavy-metal rock music and joined a group of Satan worshippers several years before this," Jolene told me. "Gradually she developed a cynical, hardened attitude, withdrawing from me and her church friends. Several times Tori tried to commit suicide. She slit her wrists, overdosed on drugs, and once jumped out of a two-story building."

Tori was born out of wedlock when Jolene herself was only a teenager. As a single mother, Jolene shared with Tori the circumstances about her birth, hoping to free her from some of the mistakes she'd made in her own teen years. But her openness seemed to have the opposite effect on her daughter.

Addicted To Rock Music

At age thirteen, Tori began listening to heavy-metal tapes and attending rock concerts. This music propagates the use of drugs, suicide, and violence. Song titles such as "Highway to Hell," "Hell Ain't a Bad Place to Be," and "Shoot to Thrill" reveal the core of their philosophy. Within a year, Tori was addicted to acid-rock music. She began doing weird chants and calling up evil spirits to do her bidding.

"When she lapsed into a spell or trance, she exhibited such supernatural strength she would beat me up," Jolene confided. "She joined a teenage group called the Black Rose Petal of Death. They sometimes met at the graveyard at night to conduct mysterious rituals which Tori refused to discuss with me."

Jolene began praying earnestly for her daughter. Others at her church joined their prayers with hers. In some ways, it seemed the situation got worse instead of better, but they persisted in prayer. Jolene tried in every way she knew to reach out to Tori in love.

One day, a fifteen-year-old boy in Tori's satanic group shot himself in the head. His suicide note read, "I hate my dad. I'm going to hell. I'm ending my life." Although Tori had attemped suicide herself, her friend's bizarre death so frightened her that she put away all her satanic practices.

"How did you deal with this matter of forgiveness?" I asked Jolene.

"I realized Tori's behavior stemmed from a broken heart," she responded. "She was punishing God and me for all the things she had gone through. When the Lord revealed to me how deeply she was hurt, I was able to forgive. That brought healing to our relationship."

Tori now works for a family as a live-in babysitter caring for their two small children. She attends church occasionally.

Disappointment has not had the final word; Jolene has stepped over that hurdle and, in faith, believes God for a complete restoration of everything the enemy has stolen from Tori and herself. "She's my prodigal child; she doesn't belong to the enemy," Jolene affirms with confidence. "She's coming home someday—to God and me."

The Anguish of Suicide

Thousands of parents suffer the trauma of losing a child to suicide, causing them not only to grieve the loss of a child, but to struggle with guilt, shame, anger, and other raw emotions which surface.

Nina has been through this experience. Her twenty-eight-year-old son Bud, the father of two children, hanged himself one Monday morning after a quarrel with his wife. She had been out all night working as a barmaid—a job he didn't want her to have. She insisted on keeping it because the tips were good and they had financial problems.

Months after the tragedy, Nina talked to her Sunday school teacher about the frustration she felt. "I don't understand why God let him do it. He could have stopped my son from killing himself!"

"Could it be that you have unforgiveness toward God for disappointing you?" the teacher asked. "Or toward your son because he chose this way of dealing with his problems?"

"I'm not aware of it," Nina responded. "But if you sense that, maybe I need to forgive both of them."

Cleansing tears—long overdue tears—began pouring down her face. "God, forgive me for holding unforgiveness toward my son for doing this. . .God, I forgive Bud," she prayed. "And Lord, I'm sorry I blamed you for his death. Please forgive me." More tears fell, and a warm, welcome peace enveloped her.

"Satan is the one who comes to steal, kill, and destroy. I know that now. It wasn't God who killed my son," she shared with me.

"It's amazing that I was unaware of the bitterness and unforgiveness I was harboring until my teacher talked to me that day," she said. "I felt such release after forgiving Bud and forgiving God. It was a starting point that drew me closer to the Lord. Eventually my husband and daughter were drawn to Him, too. Now all of us are committed to Jesus Christ; we're not just Sunday pew-sitters."

Turning Hearts To The Children
The Old Testament ends with an astounding prophecy:

174

> "See, I will send you the prophet Elijah (referring to Christ, the Messiah) before that great and dreadful day of the Lord comes. He will turn the hearts of the fathers to their children, and the hearts of the children to their fathers; or else I will come and strike the land with a curse" (Mal. 4:5,6).

While this verse has many interpretations, I believe God's desire is that the hearts of the parents be restored to their children; and the hearts of the children, to their parents. Notice: the prophet mentions first that the *parents'* hearts change. The responsibility to forgive rests squarely on our shoulders. As Dr. James Dobson says:

> It is simply not prudent to write off a son or daughter no matter how foolish, irritating, selfish or insane a child may seem to be. You need to be there not only while their canoe is bouncing precariously, but after the river runs smooth again. You have the remainder of your life to reconstruct the relationship that is now in jeopardy. Don't let anger fester for too long. Make the first move toward reconciliation. [4]

As we have seen, parents' dreams and goals for their children often diminish or are obliterated by life's obstacles or wrong choices. Parents can easily become disappointed. Adjusting to disappointment is necessary for most of us. Along with that adjustment, we find it necessary to forgive God, to forgive our children, and to forgive ourselves.

Prayer

Lord, I admit there are times when I am so disappointed in my child that I can't see anything good or positive in him/her. Forgive me for looking only at the imperfections, forgetting that I need to trust You, who does everything in the right way and at the right time. Lord, only You know the deepest needs of my child's heart; only You know when _____ 's particular situation is fully ripe for Your answer. Help me to make times of disappointment and heartache times of learning and training for future usefulness. I commit _____ into Your hands, Father; and I thank You that victory is on the way for this child. In Jesus' name I pray, with thanksgiving for all Your blessings. Amen.

Fourteen

How To Bless
Your Children

How would you respond when your youngest daughter insisted on marrying a young man with a terrible temper, someone who had caused her grief, heartache, and tears throughout the eight years of their relationship?

This was the crisis facing Jamie Buckingham, pastor of the Tabernacle Church in Melbourne, Florida, and his wife Jackie when Sandy, youngest of their five children, told them she was marrying Jerry Smith.

Jackie tells their story:

> We had given each of our older children the freedom to make their own choices, but we severely question- ed Sandy's judgment when it came to Jerry Smith, whom she had dated all the way through high school. In fact, we had done everything we could to break up their relationship.

Although Jerry was a Christian and a member of our church, his early years had not been spent in a Christian home. His Catholic parents had accepted Christ about the time Jerry entered his teens. Spirit-baptized, they were dedicated to the Lord; but those earlier, violent years had scarred their son.

Jerry was an outstanding athlete, but was impulsive, short-tempered, and often violent. At other times he and Sandy had physically battered each other, sometimes in public. This was entirely foreign to our gentle way of life, and Jamie and I were deeply concerned Sandy might become an abused wife if she married Jerry.

We met with Jerry's parents. They were equally concerned. We recommended counseling for the kids and they both submitted themselves to a friend who has a deliverance ministry. Things got better, but evidences of the old life hung on. The Smiths cooperated with us by insisting Sandy and Jerry break off their relationship for a year. Sandy went off to Oral Roberts University and Jerry attended Evangel College in Springfield, Missouri. At the end of the year, Sandy was back home. The phone bills were staggering; and the relationship, even from afar, was just as strong.

There was another year of separation when Jerry joined the U.S. Coast Guard. Jamie and I kept praying, hoping that Sandy would meet another boy; or Jerry, another girl.

Why Can't You See the Good?

"Mom," Sandy kept saying, "Why can't you see the good in Jerry that I see? Underneath that rough exterior is a real man of God. He's frightened of you and

Dad. That's the reason he seems unfriendly when he's around you."

Then one day Sandy made her announcement. "Jerry and I are going to get married. We'll not do it until you and Dad bless us, but we are going to get married."

I talked with Jamie. "We've done everything we can to break them up," he said. "Maybe God wants us to start blessing them rather than cursing them."

We looked at Matthew 18:18 together: "I tell you the truth, whatever you bind on earth will be bound in heaven, and whatever you loose on earth will be loosed in heaven."

"Let's loose them," Jamie suggested.

"OK," I agreed warily.

Jerry was to be home the next week on leave from the Coast Guard. We took the young couple out to dinner, and Jamie laid it out for them to understand. "All these years we've 'bound' you," he said. "We've done all we could to separate you. Now God has told us to 'loose' you. We are going to bless you. If you want to get married, we are going to bless that, too."

They looked at each other in amazement. Slowly Jerry's ever-present scowl turned into a grin. "You really mean it?"

"We really mean it," I said. "Jamie's parents did everything they could to keep us apart because they didn't approve of me. But when they loosed us, when they started blessing our relationship rather than cursing it, everything changed."

It was a tough decision, for in the flesh we didn't see any hope for the marriage to work out. But over the next eight months before the wedding, we watched Jerry become who Sandy had said he was all along—

a man of God. His violence, which we now realize was his only defense against our disapproval, disappeared. In its place emerged a kind, polite, Christian gentleman who has made a wonderful husband for our daughter—just as she had faith to believe." [1]

Forgiving and Loosing Go Hand In Hand

I knew the Buckinghams while they were going through their difficult years with Sandy, and I watched them forgive time and time again. The turning point came when Jamie finally said to Jackie, "Let's loose them." From then on they set Sandy and Jerry free—free of judgments, free of expectations, free to be responsible for their own choices. Forgiving and loosing—powerful, liberating "tools" in the hands of loving parents.

Sometimes we feel we've done everything we know to do to rear godly children, then we watch helplessly as they flounder into what seems to be "never-never land." We need to forgive them, but perhaps we also need to explore the possibility that they may be:

1. bound by our words and attitudes (or someone else's) and need to be loosed; or
2. adversely affected by generational weaknesses (or curses) that have surfaced in them, and they need to be set free—loosed as well as forgiven.

Both these subjects may seem unlikely. Let's consider the need for us to stand as two-in-agreement to revoke our own ill-chosen words and wrong attitudes toward our children, as Jamie and Jackie did for their daughter. We may also need to face head-on our responsibility to break hereditary influences on both sides of our family tree.

Our Words Can Bless Or Curse

Let's first consider the power of our words. Jamie recognized it was important to release Sandy with a *blessing* when he realized that binding and loosing is linked to an Old Testament concept of cursing and blessing. He believed his and Jackie's negative words and attitudes, in a sense, had cursed or bound Sandy and Jerry. What they needed was to be loosed and blessed!

Jamie recalled the incident in Deuteronomy when God told Moses to curse the enemy and bless God's people. Moses prepared the Israelites to enter the promised land by giving them God's orders:

> "See, I am setting before you today a blessing and a curse—the blessing if you obey the commands of the Lord your God...the curse if you disobey the commands of the Lord your God...by following after other gods, which you have not known" (Deut. 11:26–28).

Moses gave instructions that certain tribes were to stand on Mount Gerizim to pronounce the blessings and other designated tribes were to stand on Mount Ebal to pronounce the curses.

The people agreed with God saying, "Amen," or "So be it." They recognized that obedience would bring blessing; disobedience would cause the curses to come upon them (see Deuteronomy 27:14–26). Their *words* were binding because God says His Word stands!

Our spoken words can be like blessings or curses—to hurt or to heal. The Bible tells us, "The tongue has the power of life and death" (Prov. 18:21). Most parents have little understanding of the spiritual power inherent in the words we speak to our children —either for good or for ill. In our years of parenting, a majority of us have unintentionally cursed our children by the negative words we have spoken.

It's easy to do. In a heated moment, without thinking, we can say such things as, "You dummy! You don't have any more sense than your granddaddy." Or, "Bobby, you are lazy just like your shiftless Uncle Bob. You'll never amount to anything either." Or, "You'll never do well in math. I never did, and you're just like me."

Esteem Valuable

According to the dictionary, the word *bless* or *blessing* means to wish a person favor, wholeness, benefit, happiness, prosperity; the words occur in the Bible more than four hundred times.

The verb "to bless" in Hebrew means to bow the knee, to show reverence, or to *esteem the person valuable.* [2]

The word *curse* appears in various forms in the Bible more than 150 times. The Hebrew word translated *curse* means to make light, of little weight, to bring into contempt, to despise or to dishonor. [3]

A minister friend of mine explains that blessings and curses usually come through *words*. These words—when spoken, written, or formed inwardly and believed by the one speaking—can sometimes produce supernatural effects, either for good or for evil.

When we make a negative statement about our child, it's possible that we set in operation a "word curse." As the following illustration shows, others can curse our children in the same way.

He Is Not a Bad Boy

As Joannie walked into the church day-care center one afternoon to pick up her two-year-old son, she overheard the nursery worker say, "Bart, you are a bad, bad boy."

Joannie wasted no time telling her, "I want you to make that right with Bart. Correct his behavior, but don't let your words wound his spirit. He was wrong to take the other child's toy, and he should be told. But please, don't ever tell him he is a bad boy. He's a child of the King, and he made a mistake, but he's not a bad boy."

Bart is truly blessed! His mother understands that discipline is essential for his behavioral development, but she doesn't want him wounded by hearing that he is "bad." She wants him to grow up blessed!

Words Can Be Binding

Sometimes we parents watch, almost horrified, as our children become what they've heard spoken about them much of their lives. We see behavior habits we abhor and wonder why and how this could be.

Mona's mother, on more than one occasion, had shouted at her, "You are incorrigible, Mona. Someday you'll have a daughter who will sass you back like you do me!"

"Mom, I hate you," sixteen-year-old Mona would scream back. "You don't understand me—you don't even try. I'm going to be an understanding mom when I have kids—you wait and see!"

Mona pushed the memory of these shouting matches into the recesses of her subconscious until one afternoon at a Texas conference when she heard me tell of the necessity of breaking words spoken over us or our children. In the hotel lobby afterwards, she asked if I'd pray with her.

"My youngest daughter reacted to me like I did to my mom, and I have resented her for it," she said. "I need to get things right with her. Before Mom died, I became a Christian and went to her hospital room to ask forgiveness for my rebellious teenage years. She released me with forgiveness. I desperately need to do that for my daughter."

Revoking the Words

We prayed together and Mona forgave her daughter. She asked God for an opportunity to explain the need to "break off" her grandmother's words that had bound her.

Five months later, a jubilant Mona called me from Texas. "God answered our prayer!" she reported. "My visit with my daughter was wonderful. She was open to my praying with her. After talking for hours, we've come to a new understanding of each other. We revoked the words my mom had spoken over me—that I would have an incorrigible daughter. We also broke other curses and weaknesses passed down through our family for generations."

"Did you see results?" I asked.

"Yes, an amazing thing has happened since then," she answered. "All three of my children and my husband have recommitted their lives to the Lord! It's absolutely wonderful how He is moving in our family."

When we see the power of words that curse—that make light of or dishonor someone made in the image of God—we begin to understand how our negative words affect our children. It stirs us to change. Instead of curses, we want to impart *blessings* to them with our words.

Biblical Examples

Word curses are real, with real results. Let's look at a few biblical examples:

When Jacob and his family left his father-in-law Laban to return to Canaan, Laban pursued him to recover his household gods. Laban challenged Jacob about the missing items, and Jacob replied, "If you find anyone who has your gods, he shall not live" (Gen. 31:32). His declaration was, in effect, a "word curse." He didn't know that his own beloved wife Rachel, Laban's daughter, had taken them and was hiding them inside her camel's saddle (see Genesis 31:34,35).

Of course, Jacob did not intend to curse his own wife. But we read a few chapters later that Rachel had difficulty in giving birth and died, just as the words had been spoken (see Genesis 35:16–19).

Joshua burned the city of Jericho and declared, "Cursed before the Lord is the man who undertakes to rebuild this city, Jericho: 'At the cost of his firstborn son will he lay its foundations; at the cost of his youngest will he set up its gates' " (Josh. 6:26).

Approximately five hundred years later, when Hiel rebuilt the foundation of Jericho, his firstborn died; and when he set up the gates, his youngest died—exactly as Joshua had spoken (see I Kings 16:34).

Jesus Spoke A Curse

The cursing and blessing principle continued in the New Testament. For example, one day as Jesus was leaving Bethany, He saw a fig tree in the distance and, being hungry, looked to see if it had fruit. Finding none, he spoke to the tree, "May no one ever eat fruit from you again." The next day as the disciples were walking with Him, Peter saw the tree withered all the way to its roots and said, "The fig tree you cursed has withered" (see Mark 11:12–14,20,21).

Although Jesus did not use the word "curse" when He spoke to the tree, He did not correct Peter when he said, "The fig tree you cursed...."

We also know this was a rare example; Jesus' ministry stands out as one that constantly pointed the way to receiving His Father's blessings.

Blessing the Children

From Old Testament times to now, the tradition of the father blessing the children has been an important part of Jewish family life. It was a duty of parents to their children and has continued as a regular part of the rabbis' duties toward children on Shabat (the Sabbath) and on feast and holy days. [4] I recently visited a Jewish temple on a Friday night where a rabbi sang a blessing over all the children as they gathered at the front of the room.

In blessing children, the patriarchs attached a high value to their offspring, who in turn greatly desired their blessing. Abraham spoke a blessing to his son Isaac. Isaac blessed Jacob. Jacob blessed his twelve sons and two grandsons. [5]

Before Moses' death, he again pronounced a blessing over each individual tribe of Israel—the families, clans, all the people of God (see Deuteronomy 33).

Remember how disappointed Esau was when he let his brother Jacob rob him of the "first son" blessing? He begged his father, "Bless me—me too, my father!...haven't you reserved any blessing for me?" (Gen. 27:34,36). Esau received a blessing, but not the cherished one Isaac gave Jacob.

In biblical times, sons and daughters cherished their father's blessing. It gave them a sense of being highly valued by their parents, and they felt assured of a successful future. Today in Jewish Orthodox homes, the children still receive their father's blessings on a regular basis. [6]

Children Are Gifts from God

Why all this emphasis on blessing our children? We need to be clear on the point that children are entrusted to us from God as gifts.

"Behold, children are a gift of the Lord; The fruit of the womb is a reward" (Psa. 127:3 NASB).

One way we show our children they are accepted as gifts from God is affirming them with our blessings—which includes speaking lovingly to them. Often this can be accompanied with a hug, kiss, or touch.

When I used to see my son off to work, I'd pat him on the shoulder and give him biblical words of encouragement. "Keith, may you be a force for righteousness today." Or, "Mighty man of valor, have a good day." Or, "May God give you wisdom and great discernment on the job today." The language may have sounded stilted, but he received the impact of the blessing, nevertheless.

In biblical times, the spoken blessing was accompanied by laying hands on the children. When Joseph brought his two sons to his elderly father, Israel kissed and embraced them and stretched out his hand and blessed them with words that spoke of their future. Jesus took children in his arms, put his hands on them, and blessed them.

To bless our children involves recognizing each one's individual talents and helping each child develop in those areas. When two of our children were quite young, we discovered they liked art, so we gave them private art lessons. In college, one studied interior design; the other, graphic arts. We gave our youngest lots of books because she liked to read.

Every child needs to know that God is personally concerned with his or her life and welfare and that he or she is of infinite value to Him. Every child needs to feel that his parents regard him in this same way.

Generational Curses and Weaknesses

Society blames environment, social conditioning, or genes for wrong behavior in individuals. As Christians, we believe Adam's sin contaminated the entire human race, so that from birth we are predisposed to sin (see Romans 5:19).

Is it not possible that a curse may have been set in motion years ago by our ancestors that now influences our children to be wayward in some particular area? While we don't bear guilt for our ancestor's sins, we may sometimes suffer the consequences or results of their sin—*reaping what was sowed.*

For example, after King David committed adultery with Bathsheba, the prophet Nathan warned him:

> "This is what the Lord says: 'Out of your own household I am going to bring calamity upon you. Before your very eyes I will take your wives and give them to one who is close to you, and he will lie with your wives in broad daylight. You did it in secret, but I will do this thing in broad daylight before all Israel' " (2 Sam. 12:11,12).

His son Absalom fulfilled exactly what God had said (see 2 Samuel 16:22); and another son, Solomon, took hundreds of heathen wives who turned his heart from God (see 1 Kings 11:1–4). Although God forgave David when he repented, the consequences of David's sin plagued him and his household.

Uncontrollable Compulsion

Consider the example of a child unable to control himself from stealing. He may insist he doesn't want to behave the way he does, and he may really try to stop it, but he has an uncontrollable compulsion to steal. It could well be that he is, as we've mentioned previously, (1) under the power of word curses spoken over him, or (2) under a generational curse or weakness passed down through his ancestors. The child's inherent bent to sin manifests itself through stealing.

How often we see a pattern of behavior—promiscuity, for example—repeated in a family. We may tend to think of promiscuity as learned behavior, looseness, or even poor role modeling. In fact, it could be a curse traceable to ancestors who were rebellious toward God.

An End to the Sin Pattern

A mother whom I'll call Carla shared with me that she had had three abortions while she was in high school. Just before she turned nineteen, she married and gave birth to a son and a daughter. Years later, after she had accepted Jesus as Lord of her life, she went to her daughter Andrea to talk about her past.

First, Carla asked Andrea to forgive her because at one time she had not wanted children and had aborted three babies. "Of course, I forgive you, Mother," Andrea responded, falling against Carla's shoulder. "You were brave enough to have me, weren't you? And you were a good mother."

As they talked, Andrea confessed that her grandfather—Carla's father—had often molested her during her teenage years. Carla then told Andrea that her own grandfather—her father's father—had sexually molested her.

The more they talked, the more they realized a need to break the generational curse that had passed down in their family through sexual immorality. Together they prayed, declaring an end to the sin pattern. They confessed their own sin of bitterness and asked God to forgive those who had sinned against them.

Carla went to her elderly father and told him she knew he had sexually abused Andrea and that both of them had forgiven him. Did he have anything to say? He broke down weeping. Hard as that meeting was, Carla's honesty bore fruit. That day, her father accepted Jesus as his Savior.

Next, Carla visited her son and asked for his forgiveness, just as she had asked for Andrea's. He too released her with loving words of forgiveness.

Parents must use discretion and sensitivity in confessing to their children the sins of their past. When prompted by the Holy Spirit—especially in areas where the parents need to ask the child's forgiveness or offer forgiveness to the child—such confessions can bring deliverance and healing.

Obedience Is Critical

Blessings, as we see from the Bible, come through obeying God. Generational curses *usually* take effect because of disobedience—whether active or passive—on the part of the believer. Many Old Testament curses resulted from idolatry, dishonoring parents, stealing, injustice, illicit or unnatural sex, murder, or bribery (see Deuteronomy 27).

Some Bible teachers believe curses also come through supernaturally empowered representatives of Satan. These followers of Satan may well release evil power into the lives of others through curses which they speak, write, or utter inwardly. Again, disobedience is usually the cause for a believer being vulnerable to such curses.

Wait a minute. Didn't Jesus destroy the works of the devil and redeem me from the curse?

Yes, He did. The apostle Paul writes,

> "Christ redeemed us from the curse of the law by becoming a curse for us, for it is written: 'Cursed is everyone who is hung on a tree.' He redeemed us in order that the blessing given to Abraham might come to the Gentiles through Christ Jesus" (Gal. 3:13,14).

He redeemed us, but *we* need to *apply* that redemptive provision and appropriate His forgiveness. We must walk in obedience to be assured of God's protection. As Christians, we have the power to break a curse and to prevent its effect from continuing. We do it by:

1. Confessing our sins of rebellion and disobedience, as well as the sins of our forefathers;
2. Receiving and appropriating God's forgiveness;
3. Thanking Jesus that because we've accepted Him as Savior, His blood cleanses us and frees us from the sins of our forefathers;
4. Declaring defeat to the enemy through binding and loosing.

The Power of Binding and Loosing

Jesus taught this important principle of binding and loosing that applies to *all* His followers:

> "I will give you the keys of the kingdom of heaven; whatever you bind on earth will be bound in heaven, and whatever you loose on earth will be loosed in heaven" (Matt. 16:19).

The Williams translation of the New Testament points out that the verb form of *bind* and *loose* indicates something "in a state of having been already forbidden." [7] Thus, whatever we bind or loose in accordance with God's will has already been bound or loosed in heaven.

Jesus also said, "How can anyone enter a strong man's house and carry off his possessions unless he first ties up the strong man? Then he can rob his house" (Matt. 12:29). The context of this passage is an instance where Jesus was casting out demons.

The Greek word for *bind* in these verses means "to fasten or tie—as with chains," as an animal is tied to keep it under control. [8] As believing parents, we have the authority through Jesus (in fact, the *responsibility)* to bind evil, harassing spirits and command them to cease operating in the lives of our children.

To what does the loosing refer? To setting captives free! The Greek word for *loose* means "to loose anything tied or fastened; to loose one bound; to set free; to discharge from prison. Also, to free from bondage or disease (one held by Satan) by restoration to health. [9]

Consider the incident of Jesus healing the woman crippled by a spirit for eighteen years. "Woman, you are set free from your infirmity," He told her (Luke 13:12). He loosed her from the power of the evil spirit, and she was restored to health.

As we become diligent in our "binding and loosing" prayers over our children, we can see them released from the bondage of the enemy, free to be blessed by God's love.

Share Your Weaknesses

Some Christians do not believe that Satan's evil forces can oppress their lives, especially through several generations. Yet other Christians, who research their family history and find things they know were displeasing to God, simply bind those evil spirits off their families with tangible results. Charlotte, who had struggled with thoughts of suicide, did this when she discovered three generations of suicide in her own family.

I know parents who feel it is beneficial to sit down with their children and share the weaknesses they themselves have struggled with. They also share problems—such as alcoholism—which have been prevalent in the family line. This accomplishes two things: 1) It alerts the children to the possibility that the same problems could show up in their lives, and 2) It provides parents opportunity to teach their children the principle of binding and loosing.

One family recognized their need to bind infidelity from operating in their family. Lois' father had been unfaithful to his wife; his two sons were unfaithful to their wives. In Lois' research she discovered that her grandfather, who had been adopted, was born out of wedlock. Three generations had practiced sexual sin.

Lois, her husband, and their children prayed together and broke that generational curse so that the tendency to illicit sex would not continue to be passed down in their family. Lois told her sister what they had done, so that she could pray with her family in a similar manner.

Jesus gave us authority to bind the work of the enemy in our families and to see his victims set free—released by the greater power of God. We must put forth the effort to use the "keys of the kingdom" Jesus made available to us.

Forgiveness and loosing—they go hand in hand because they produce the same effect.

Let's pray now to revoke any curses that may have bound our children, whether spoken or written word curses or generational sins and curses passed down to them.

Prayer of Confession and Repentance

Lord Jesus Christ, I acknowledge You as the Son of God, and I thank You for dying on the cross for my sins. You redeemed me from the curse of sin that I might receive Your blessings.

Father, forgive and cleanse any sin committed by me or my ancestors that exposed our family to a curse even to the third, fourth or tenth generation. I repent of these sins and renounce all disobedience and cooperation with evil spirits.

Thank You that my family is freed from past bondages and that You will restore what the enemy has stolen. I love You, Lord. I praise You, Lord. I worship You, my Savior.

Binding the Enemy

Satan, I bind you and all your evil forces that have come against our family through word curses or generational sins. By the power and authority of Jesus Christ of Nazareth, I declare that the curse is broken and your power is bound off my children and entire family. I command you to release us from all harrassment.

You have no authority in this family because we are covered by the blood of Jesus, the Son of God. By His power and in His name, I declare null and void any curses of deception, poverty, infirmity, promiscuity, adultery, abuse, perversion, illegitimacy, mental or emotional oppression, violence, fear, rebellion, addictions, murder, suicide or [name any others the Holy Spirit reveals to you].

In Jesus' name, I bind your evil power that is controlling the will of _____ to prevent him/her from freely choosing to walk in obedience to God's Word. I serve notice on all your foul, unclean spirits that Jesus' blood cleanses and protects us.

Prayer Of Loosing

Lord, I ask You to release the power of the Holy Spirit to bring conviction, a full revelation of truth, and escape from the snare of the devil. Bring to his/her senses and draw him/her to repentance and reconcilation with God, the Father.

I ask You, Lord God, to release a spirit of peace over my family, and to release Your angels to protect us and keep us. I pray in the name of Jesus, who always causes us to triumph in Him. Amen.

Blessing Prayer

Father, I speak the blessings of obedience over my family:

We will be blessed in the city and blessed in the country. Our children and all progeny will be blessed, and our means of livelihood will be blessed. Our sustenance and all necessary provisions will be blessed. We will be blessed when we come in and blessed when we go out (based on Deuteronomy 28:2-6).

I also speak Aaron's priestly blessing over my family:

"The Lord bless you and keep you; the Lord make his face shine upon you and be gracious to you; the Lord turn his face toward you and give you peace" (Num. 6:22). Amen.

Fifteen

Forgive—Then
Keep On Praying

Doctors advocate "preventive medicine"—a practice aimed at preventing sickness, rather than waiting to treat it after it strikes.

Praying is not, strictly speaking, preventive medicine. Yet in a sense, it is. After forgiving our children, we must continue to pray for them and become even more alert to the enemy's traps that so easily ensnare them. I'd much rather pray and avert problems in my children's lives, than wait until a crisis arises and then begin to pray.

My husband LeRoy and I raised all our children in a Christian home and took them to church from the time they were infants. Yet when they reached their college years, all three ventured into "the land of the enemy." I remember that precarious period when our pastor's wife encouraged us to never give up trusting God for our children. In our anxiety, she reminded us of God's promise that if we had trained our children in the way they should go, when they are old they will not depart from it (see Proverbs 22:6).

In the twenty-nine years we've been parents, we've learned volumes about forgiveness and prayer. Needless to say, we've had many opportunities to forgive our three children. There have been plenty of times when we've had to ask them to forgive us, too. Through it all, we discovered our lifeline—prayer.

Prayer Pilgrimage

My prayer pilgrimage began when the children were young. Like a miner seeking gold, I searched the Bible looking for everything God said about prayer. I listened to pastors, leaders, and godly women as they talked to God. I even wrote down some of their prayers. I was after something big—getting hold of God and seeing my prayers answered. In pressing in, I discovered some invaluable principles for effective praying.

First of all, I learned to *pray specifically*—specific prayers get specific answers. I learned to *pray in agreement* with my husband and my prayer partners on a regular basis. I learned to *pray the Scriptures* to battle against the enemy's attacks on my children. I kept a prayer journal of my petitions and God's answers. I tell about this journal in *How to Pray for Your Children* (available from Aglow Publications).

For years, I prayed for my children to have godly friends, godly influences, and godly environment. I also prayed for the right friends to come into their lives at the right time. In my prayer log, I kept pictures of my children and names and pictures of some of their friends who, I knew, would influence them either positively or negatively.

Your Children Will Return

Looking back, it seems like I spent months travailing in prayer during the time my children were not serving God. During this time, God began speaking with me about each of them. I remember what happened in our younger daughter's life when we were on a trip to the Holy Land.

LeRoy and I were clearing customs in the Tel Aviv airport when I saw a huge wall banner showing Jewish people from all walks of life climbing up the mountain to the temple in Jerusalem. The scripture verse on the banner was a promise God had given me for my children:

"Restrain your voice from weeping and your eyes from tears, for your work will be rewarded," declares the Lord. "They will return from the land of the enemy. So there is hope for your future," declares the Lord. "Your children will return to their own land" (Jer. 31:16,17).

Hope! It bubbled up like a spring in my heart when I read the beautiful banner. "Yes, my children *will* return to our own land from the land of the enemy," I affirmed. "Even as the Jews are being drawn from all over the world to the nation of Israel, so my wandering children—mine and others like them—will return to the Lord."

On a cool February Sunday, LeRoy and I went to pray at the Western Wall—also called the Wailing Wall—he on the men's side, I on the women's. What an experience! We cried out to God on behalf of our three children, much as we'd interceded at our own "wailing wall" in our bedroom at home in Florida.

In the States, a few hours later that same day, Sherry, a senior at Florida State University, was preparing to drive the 125 miles from our home back to campus. A blinding rainstrom delayed her trip, so she drove only as far as the little church we attended. After circling the building three times, she pulled into the parking lot and went inside.

A visiting pastor from Africa spoke passionately on Matthew 6:33: "But seek first his kingdom and his righteousness, and all these things will be given to you as well." He challenged his hearers to find God's will for their lives and to obey it. Touched deeply, Sherry began weeping.

"You've Got to Make a Choice"

Steve, a friend of Sherry's brother, slipped into the pew beside her. Gently, but firmly, he issued a warning. "Sherry, God's not going to put up with your having one foot in the world and one foot in His Kingdom. You've got to make a choice soon. I hope it will be tonight."

Sherry broke down. Tears gushed down her face. The battle was over; the Good Shepherd had found our little lamb while we were in Israel. He wooed her back to the fold through Steve, a long-time family friend.

The following weekend, back from our trip, we visited Sherry, at her request, and attended church together. After the service, Sherry asked us to go to the altar and kneel with her. With her arms wrapped around us, she asked us to forgive her for all her rebellious ways and the years of opposing God's plan for her life. We wept together, assuring her of our forgiveness. Looking directly into her eyes, LeRoy and I each asked her to forgive us, too, for not being the parents we should have been and for failing her so often. She forgave her parents.

Right on Schedule

We still marvel at the way God chose to answer our prayers. Steve was one of the young men in the church for whom I'd prayed regularly. In fact, I'd kept his picture in my prayer journal and for eight years prayed for him every Friday while he attended Bible school and served the Lord in Greece, Germany, and Israel.

What a worthwhile investment of time and effort! He became the instrument God used to minister to our daughter. God answered our prayers to send godly friends into Sherry's life at the right time through a rainstorm and an old friend. He is so faithful!

Sherry graduated from Florida State and enrolled in a Bible school where she met and married a young man from Denmark. After they graduated, they moved to Copenhagen to do missions work. How grateful we are that the Lord kept encouraging us during those difficult years.

My Responsibility

Our other two, Keith and Quinett, came back to the Lord within a year of Sherry's return. They enrolled in a Bible institute in Dallas. Quinett has already served the Lord in Israel and Germany. Keith, a graphic artist, and Quinett, a commercial interior designer, enjoy working together to design and create sacred banners as visual worship aids. Their banners are used in South Africa, Israel, Germany, Sweden, Denmark, Norway, and in various churches and homes in the United States.

One of our responsibilities is to *pray* and *believe* God answers prayer—not boxing Him in as to the way He will answer or the person He will use. Although our children are now adults, my husband and I continue to pray for them.

Specific and Persistent

We must pay a price to see our children come into His Kingdom. Jesus clearly taught that *believing* and *forgiveness* are requisites to having our prayers answered (see Mark 11:24,25).

He also taught the importance of *specific requests* and *persistence* in prayer (see Luke 11:5-8). In this example, Jesus told the parable of a man who wakes his neighbor at midnight asking for three loaves of bread for his guests. He made a specific request, he was persistent in asking, and his request was granted.

Jesus concluded the parable by saying:

> "So I say to you: Ask and it will be given to you; seek and you will find; knock and the door will be opened to you. For everyone who asks received; he who seeks finds; and to him who knocks, the door will be opened" (Luke 11:9,10).

Why do we keep praying?

1. Because we need to guard our minds so the enemy cannot bring up again the things we've forgiven;
2. So we don't fall into unforgiveness when another situation arises;
3. So we become inwardly strengthened to walk in love;
4. To be alert to the snare the enemy would try to set for our children and to pull down his strongholds.

Single Parents

It is important—and biblical—to pray for your children in agreement with someone. If you are a single parent, ask God to provide the right prayer partner so you can agree in prayer on a regular basis.

Choose someone of your same sex with whom you feel a unity of spirit, and someone who can pray with you consistently, even if it's on the telephone. It might be another single parent; what a joy for the two of you to pray in agreement for each other's children.

Labor Before Birth

Intercession is often compared to the birthing process: conception, gestation, labor, and ultimately delivery. Unfortunately, many parents give up on intercession too quickly; they've waited and waited, prayed and prayed, and nothing seems to happen. Someone has said, "Waiting is a greenhouse where doubts flourish." How true. As time goes on, parents can be overwhelmed by doubts that things will ever change. Let me illustrate what I mean.

Labor was a new and frightening experience for me with Quinett, my first child. I'd had heavy labor pains off and on for two days and nights in a rural hospital that was greatly understaffed. On the third morning, a Sunday, I packed my bag and waddled out of the hospital. I was ready to quit.

I was standing beside U.S. Highway One when LeRoy and Mother drove up to visit me. "What in the world are you doing out here?" he asked, pulling the car into a parking slot beside the orange grove where I was standing.

"I'm tired of going through labor," I answered. "I've decided I'm not going to have this baby. Take me home."

Patiently, he took my suitcase in one hand and my arm in the other. "Honey, you can't quit now," he said, guiding me back into the hospital, past the nursing station, and down the hall to my room. "Go back and labor just a little more. The baby will come."

No one noticed that I'd left or that I was back. My doctor came in and told LeRoy and my mother that he needed their help. He was short of nurses, and he had to induce labor. I still remember that intense pain! At times, it took both LeRoy and Mother to hold me on the bed. We labored together, pushing, encouraging, fighting for the baby's birth. Six hours later, our eight-and-a-half pound daughter came into the world—bruised, red, and crying, far from beautiful, but healthy.

An enormous struggle—yes! But what a rich reward we had in the birth of our precious baby!

Don't Quit Now

Labor always precedes birth—sometimes long, hard labor. So, don't give up, parents!

As a friend of mine says, "Too many people have the attitude, 'If God doesn't answer prayer by Tuesday, then forget it!' " They don't realize there are stages in prayer, just as in "birthing" a child: *conception* (when their prayer becomes one with God's desire); *gestation* (when God enlarges the vision of His plan and they have faith to pray for it); and *labor* (travailing and believing). Only then does *birthing* take place.

I implore you, parents, don't stop now. Fight for your family. Nehemiah says it better:

"Remember the Lord, who is great and awesome, and fight for your brothers, your sons and your daughters, your wives and your homes" (Neh. 4:14).

Conflict in the Spiritual World

The Bible is clear about conflict in the spiritual world and its effect on us. Too few Christians realize that our struggle is not against flesh and blood—our children, spouses, parents, or neighbors—but "against the devil's schemes...against the rulers, against the authorities, against the powers of this dark world and against the spiritual forces of evil in the heavenly realms" (Eph. 6:11,12).

These forces of darkness hinder the truth of the gospel. They blind and deceive our children's minds. Paul wrote, "The god of this age has blinded the minds of unbelievers, so that they cannot see the light of the gospel of the glory of Christ, who is the image of God" (2 Cor. 4:4).

We are warned to be on the alert because the devil, our adversary, seeks to devour or destroy us. The devil is called the adversary, the accuser, the father of lies, a deceiver, ruler of demons, the dragon or serpent, one who comes to steal, kill, and destroy. [1]

Satan, at his highest before the fall, was only an angel. He has never been an all-knowing, all-powerful spiritual being. We sometimes forget this in the midst of a spiritual battle and give him more credit than is his due. While we are to be *aware* of the devil's schemes and tactics, we are admonished to "fix our eyes on Jesus, the author and perfecter of our faith" (Heb. 12:2). In other words, *keep your eyes on the Answer,* not on the problem.

Weapons of Warfare

The good news is that Jesus, the Son of God, came to earth to destroy the works of the devil. Jesus defeated Satan at the cross, and the Father has put *all things* under His feet. Jesus tells His followers to exercise authority over the power of the enemy until His return. He assures us that our weapons of warfare are mighty in God for pulling down enemy strongholds. [2]

Following are some of the weapons available to Christians as they pray and battle against the enemy:

The name of Jesus	Mark 16:17,18; Luke 10:17
The blood of Jesus	Heb. 9:12–14; Rev. 12:11
Agreement	Ecc. 4:9,10; Matt. 18:19,20
Binding and Loosing	Matt. 16:19; Mark 3:27
Fasting	Isa. 58:6; Matt. 6:16–18
Praise	2 Chron. 20:14–22; Psa. 149:6–9
Word and Testimony	Eph. 6:17; Heb. 4:12; Rev. 12:11

I remember the days I walked the floor battling in the unseen realm for my children's deliverance. Following Jesus' example (Matt. 4:4,7,10), I spoke aloud, "Be gone, Satan, for it is written..." and I prayed various scriptures, such as "the seed of the righteous shall be delivered...My children shall be taught of the Lord, and great will be their peace...Thank you, Lord, that you will give your angels charge over my child to guard him in all his ways." [3]

Successful Battle Plan

We have no power over men and their wills. We do have Jesus' power-of-attorney, so to speak, to bind the evil forces or powers influencing people against God's will. Jesus said what we bind on earth will be bound in heaven, and what we loose on earth will be loosed in heaven (Matt. 16:19).

An example of this principle is the case of the mother and grandparents of a runaway girl in Florida who decided to do spiritual warfare every afternoon on the girl's behalf.

"Remember that spiritual warfare on behalf of another does not control that person's will," their pastor instructed. "It does bind the power of evil forces affecting that person's will and releases the individual to make decisions freely."

Every day they declared aloud: "You evil spirits seeking to lead astray and destroy our child, Cynthia, we bind you in the name of Jesus Christ. We are seated together with Christ in spiritual authority, and we tell you to take your hands off Cynthia's life. Release her will, so she may be free to accept Jesus Christ as Savior, Lord, Deliverer, and Baptizer."

Then they prayed, "Holy Spirit of God, draw our child from the camp of the enemy. Thank You, Lord, for placing a hedge of protection about her."

After a few weeks of praying this way, the girl returned home. One of the first things she said to her mother was, "Tell me about Jesus."

As the grandmother told me this story, she explained, "You see, when the enemy was bound and her will was loosed or released, she chose to follow the Lord. Today she is walking with Him." [4]

Almost every Christian family I know is under spiritual attack. The enemy is out to capture our children and destroy our homes. But Spirit-led Christians are learning how to take back what he has stolen.

God Is for Families

In the midst of the battling, it is comforting to remember that God considers families important. Before he called a nation, he created a family. Throughout the Bible, we see His special concern for families.

When Israel was preparing to leave Egypt, each family sacrificed a lamb to cover their household. They sprinkled the blood on the doorpost in order to be spared when the death angel passed by (see Exodus 12).

God chose to send His Son to be born into a family here on earth. Jesus knew what it was like to share household chores, live with brothers who didn't understand him, and be the elder son to his widowed mother. As a youngster, he no doubt knew what it was like to be under the authority of an earthly father who wasn't His own. He became our sacrificial Lamb and shed His blood to cover our family's sins.

God ordained the family. He is restoring families today, using His divine order and lines of authority in the process.

I believe He is calling us to station ourselves as intercessory sentries, to be watchguards in prayer over our families, seeking His battle plan to thwart the enemy's schemes. The most rewarding thing we can do after forgiving our children is to pray that they will move into God's plan and purpose for their lives.

As parent after parent in this book has shown us, unforgiveness and bitterness erode family relationships. Our challenge is to forgive our children's offenses in order to receive forgiveness and restoration ourselves. If we don't forgive, we are not forgiven. Our lines of communication with God are impaired by our sin.

If we are to be the first line of defense for our children against the enemy, we must do two things: walk in love toward them and pray fervently for them. There has never been a more critical time for parents to be forgiving, loving, and praying people. We have a faithful Heavenly Father to see us through this high calling.

Prayer

Lord, thank You that You are a faithful God, keeping Your covenant of love to a thousand generations of those who love You and keep Your commands. We know our part is to pray; Your covenant is to answer. How we thank You that You are a covenant-keeping God, faithful and true. Teach us how to pray more effectively as we "stand in the gap" in faith, praying and believing and forgiving our offspring—just as You have forgiven us. In Jesus name. Amen.

Epilogue

The final weeks of work on this book happened to fall during the Thanksgiving and Christmas holiday season. While pondering the variety of situations covered here, I realized what a critical family issue forgiveness can be during the holidays.

How many thousands of people dread this season of the year? Even among Christians, who have every reason to enjoy celebrating Christ's birth, I often hear people say, "I dread Christmas this year." It may be because of hurtful memories from childhood, estrangement from family members, favoritism and sibling rivalry, the ingratitude of children, problems with a former spouse over custody of children, or a hundred other unpleasantries associated with what should be a joyful holiday.

Many psychologists' and counselors' appointment calendars are full with an increased client load at this time of year. Some place ads in local newspapers, promising to help depressed, frustrated clients make it through the holidays.

As I was having a quiet breakfast one morning in November, a question came to mind: Suppose all those people who are dreading the holidays could forgive the individuals who wounded them and those who have perpetrated the hurts would be willing to apologize and ask for forgiveness? Wouldn't that remove the spectre-like overtones which often obscure the joy of the holidays?

It may seem to be an overly simplistic solution, but the Scriptures clearly teach that forgiveness is essential to reconciliation and restoration of broken relationships.

Of course, it is not in our power to cause another person to apologize and seek forgiveness from us. But conducting our own personal "attitude check-up" is something each of us can and should do. We should be as diligent about getting rid of unforgiveness in our hearts as a cardiologist would be about dealing with plaque in our arteries. One is as great a threat to our spiritual health as the other is to our physical health.

How tragic to hear of a young man being stricken in the prime of life with deadly heart disease, often a treatable condition he was unaware of. Even more tragic is a person of any age who has allowed unforgiveness to corrode his soul and poison his spirit, while defending his right to bear a grudge. That kind of corrosion kills one's spiritual life and also affects one's physical well-being.

My prayer is that this book has helped hurting people—especially parents—release their animosities, choose to forgive, and receive the inner peace which only comes from the Prince of Peace.

Ruthanne Garlock
Dallas, Texas

End Notes

Chapter One

1. JoAnne Sekowsky, *Forgiveness, A Two-Way Street* (Lynnwood, Wa.: Aglow Publications, 1985), p. 4. Used with permission of Aglow Publications.
2. Ibid., pp. 5,6.
3. W. E. Vine, *An Expository Dictionary of New Testament Words* (Old Tappan, N.J.: Fleming Revell, 1966), p. 463.
4. Charles Stanley, *Forgiveness* (Nashville: Thomas Nelson, 1987), pp. 21,22. Copyright by Charles Stanley. Used with permission of Thomas Nelson Publishers.
5. Dr. Richard P. Walters, *Anger — Yours, and Mine and What To Do About It* (Grand Rapids: Zondervan, 1981), p. 82. Used with permission of Dr. Richard P. Walters.

Chapter Two

1. Corrie ten Boom, *Tramp For the Lord* (Grand Rapids: Fleming Revell, 1974), pp. 179,180. Copyright by Corrie ten Boom and Jamie Buckingham. Used by permission of Fleming H. Revell Company.
2. The Reverend Everett Fullam, "Holiness," in *Charisma* Magazine, January 1988, p. 67. Reprinted from *Riding The Wind* by Everett L. Fullam, 1986. Used by permission of Creation House, Altamonte Springs, FL 32714.

Chapter Three

1. James H. Strong, *Strong's Exhaustive Concordance* (Nashville: Bible Crusade Publishers), #630 Greek ref., p. 14.
2. Ibid., #5091 Greek, p. 72.
3. Anonymous, "Incest: The Family Secret," *The Last Days* Magazine, Jan.–Feb. 1985, p. 13. Copyright 1985 Last Days Ministries, Box 40, Lindale, TX 75771-0040. All Rights Reserved. Excerpts of this article were reprinted from *The Last Days* Magazine. If you would like copies of the com-

plete article in booklet form, please write to Last Days Ministries at the above address and ask for BL #70. Used with permission.

4. Ibid., p. 14.
5. Ibid.
6. Gary Smalley & John Trent, Ph.d., *The Gift of Honor* (Nashville: Thomas Nelson, 1987) p. 33. Copyright by Gary Smalley and John Trent, Ph.d. Used with permission of Thomas Nelson Publishers.

Chapter Four

1. Peter Lord, *Hearing God* (Grand Rapids: Baker Book House, 1988) pp. 75, 76. Used with permission of Baker Book House.
2. Mary Rae Deatrick, *Easing the Pain of Parenthood* (Portland: Harvest House, 1979), p. 40. Used with permission of Mary Rae Deatrick, San Diego, CA 92120.

Chapter Five

1. Charles Stanley, Op. Cit., p. 81.
2. Alfred Edersheim, *The Life and Times of Jesus, the Messiah* (Grand Rapids: Eerdman's, 1965), p. 260.
3. *New International Version Study Bible* (Grand Rapids: Zondervan, 1985), p. 1569.
4. Ibid., p. 1570.

Chapter Six

1. Helen Hosier, *You Never Stop Being A Parent* (Old Tappan, N.J.: Fleming Revell, 1986), p. 52. Copyright by Helen Hosier. Used by permission of Fleming H. Revell Company.
2. Ibid., p. 53.

Chapter Seven

1. Myrle Carner, "Seven Things Teens Are Dying to Tell Their Parents," 1988 Seattle Police Statistics, published in *Focus on the Family* Magazine, May 1988, p. 12.
2. Richard P. Walters, Op. Cit., p. 81.
3. Josh McDowell and Dick Day, *Why Wait? What You Need to Know About the Teen Sexuality Crisis* (San Bernardino: Here's Life Publishers, 1987), p. 412. Used with permission of Here's Life Publishers, San Bernardino, CA 92402.
4. Ibid.
5. Ibid., p. 413.
6. Ibid., p. 415.
7. Ibid., pp. 416–418.
8. Penny Lea, *Rachel Weeping;* 1987 Pamphlet by I Believe in Life, P.O. Box 34077, Pensacola, FL 32507.

Chapter Eight

1. Margie M. Lewis with Gregg Lewis, *The Hurting Parent* (Grand Rapids: Zondervan, 1980) p. 103. Copyright 1980, 1988 by Margie M. Lewis and Gregg Lewis. Used by permission of Zondervan Publishing House.
2. Ibid., pp. 103, 104.
3. Michael R. Saia, *Counseling the Homosexual* (Minneapolis: Bethany House, 1988), p. 85. Used by permission of Bethany House Publishers, Minneapolis, MN 55438.
4. Ibid., p. 49.
5. Ibid., pp. 57, 58.
6. Article from *Daily News,* Fort Walton Beach, FL, Dec. 10, 1985, and from Mike Williams' testimony tape. Testimony used by permission of Mike Williams, P.O. Box 572, Olney, IL 62450.
7. Jerry Arterburn with Steve Arterburn, *How Will I Tell My Mother?* (Nashville: Oliver-Nelson, 1988), pp. 95, 96. Used by permission of Oliver-Nelson Publishers, Nashville, TN.

8. Ibid., pp. 105, 106.
9. Ibid., p. 115.
10. Ibid., p. 148.
11. Ibid., pp. xi, xii.

Chapter Nine

1. Dr. David J. and Bonnie B. Juroe, *Successful Step-Parenting* (Old Tappan, N.J.: Power Books, Fleming Revell, 1983), pp. 9, 19. Copyright 1983 by David J. Juroe and Bonnie Buzzell Juroe. Used with permission of Fleming H. Revell Company.
2. Ibid., pp. 20–27.
3. Ibid., p. 28.
4. Ibid., p. 35.
5. W.E. Vine, Op. Cit., p. 21.

Chapter Ten

1. Herbert Lockyer, Sr., General Editor, *Nelson's Illustrated Bible Dictionary* (Nashville: Thomas Nelson, 1986), p. 20.

Chapter Eleven

1. Dr. Robert Wallace, " 'Tween 12 and 20" column, *Daily News,* Fort Walton Beach, FL, June 16, 1988.
2. Jamie Buckingham, *The Trumpet* Newsletter, September 22, 1988.
3. Ibid.
4. David Barton, *America: To Pray or Not to Pray?* (Aledo: Specialty Research Associates, 1988), p. 102. Used by permission of Specialty Research Associates, Inc., P.O. Box 397, Aledo, TX 76008.
5. Jay Strack, *Drugs and Drinking* (Nashville: Thomas Nelson, 1985), p. 17. Used by permission of Thomas Nelson Publishers, Nashville, TN.

6. Ibid.
7. Ibid., pp. 182–187.

Chapter Twelve

1. J. I. Packer, Merrill C. Tenney, William White, Jr., *The Bible Almanac* (New York: Guideposts, by special arrangement with Thomas Nelson Publishers, 1980) p. 415.

Chapter Thirteen

1. Debbie Hedstrom, "A Mom's Secret Weapon: Forgiveness," *Aglow* Magazine, December 1987. Used with permission.
2. "Expert Explains Mental Retardation," *The United Methodist Reporter,* December 2, 1988.
3. Greg Reid, "Where I Live," *Bloodline Ministries Newsletter* (El Paso, TX), November, 1988.
4. Dr. James Dobson, *Parenting Isn't For Cowards* (Dallas: Word Books, 1987), p. 155. Used with permission of Word Books.

Chapter Fourteen

1. Jackie Buckingham, "Healing the Wounded Heart" in *Help! I'm a Pastor's Wife* (Altamonte Springs, FL: Creation House, 1987), pp. 259–262. Edited by Michelle Buckingham. Used with permission of Creation House and Jackie Buckingham.
2. Gary Smalley and John Trent, Ph.D., *The Blessing* (Nashville: Thomas Nelson, 1986), p. 26. Copyright by Gary Smalley and John Trent. Used with permission of Thomas Nelson Publishers.
3. James H. Strong, Op. Cit., #7043 Hebrew reference, p. 103.
4. Gary Smalley and John Trent, *The Blessing,* p. 30.
5. Ibid., p. 26.
6. Ibid., pp. 30, 33.
7. Charles B. Williams, *The New Testament in the Language of the People* (Chicago: Moody Press, 1966), p. 47.

8. Joseph Henry Thayer, *A Greek-English Lexicon of the New Testament* (Grand Rapids: Baker Book House, 1977), p. 384.
9. Ibid.

Chapter Fifteen
1. 1 Pet. 5:8; Rev. 12:10; 2 Cor. 11:14; Job 15:21; John 8:44; Gen. 3:13; Matt. 12:24; Rev. 12:9 & 20:2; John 10:10.
2. 1 John 3:8; Eph. 1:22; Luke 10:19; 2 Cor. 10:4.
3. Prov. 11:21; Isa. 54:13; Psa. 91:11.
4. Barbara Joseph, Interview with Quin Sherrer on her book, *How to Pray For Your Children, Aglow* Magazine, December 1987. Used with permission.